Oath of Allegiance.

I, *Pauline Vincent Turner*

swear by Almighty God that I will be faithful and bear true allegiance to His Majesty, King George the Fifth, His Heirs and Successors, according to law.

(Signature of Alien) *Pauline Vincent Turner*

Sworn and subscribed this 25th day of *January* 1928, before me,

(Signature) *M. Greenwood*

M.G. ~~Justice of the Peace for~~

A Commissioner for Oaths.

Address { 32 Ely Place
Holborn E.C.1

2 FEB 1928

Unless otherwise indicated hereon, if the Oath of Allegiance is not taken within one calendar month after the date of this Certificate, the Certificate shall not take effect

A MINK COAT IN ST NEOTS

A Mink Coat in St Neots

My Mother's Flower Shop and the mystery of a wealthy Russian Princess

LIZ HODGKINSON

Anthony Eyre
MOUNT ORLEANS PRESS

Frontispiece: sketch of Pauline by Alex Williams

Published in Great Britain in 2024
by Anthony Eyre, Mount Orleans Press
23 High Street, Cricklade SN6 6AP
https://anthonyeyre.com

ISBN 978-1-912945-49-8

A CIP record for this book is available
from the British Library

Set in 11/15pt Joanna Nova

Printed in Malta by
Gutenberg Press

To Susan Dorey

'one of us'

Contents

I

How it all started

IN JANUARY 2016, I was sitting on a mountain top at a spiritual retreat centre in Mount Abu, India, enjoying a cup of tea with two English guests, the former PR guru Lynne Franks and another woman who introduced herself as Liz Edmunds.

I knew Lynne Franks well as we had first met in 1973 when I was a fashion writer on the *Sunday People* newspaper, and she had just started her PR business. She has been high-profile and something of a celebrity ever since. But as Liz Edmunds was unknown to me, I asked in somewhat queenly tones where she came from.

'A little place you will never have heard of,' she replied.

'Try me,' I said.

She hesitated for a moment, and then said: 'Great Staughton.' She sounded confident enough that I would, as she predicted, never have heard of the place. But—I had. I said: 'What? I don't believe it. I've come all the way to India to be sitting next to somebody from Great Staughton?'

Liz asked in astonishment: 'Do you know it, then?'

'Not only do I know it, I can describe it to you exactly. It consists of one long narrow street with houses each side and a church round the corner.' I went on: 'I know it because I was born and grew up in St Neots, about five miles outside Great Staughton, and often used to visit the village. There used to be a Post Office just as you entered the village.'

'That has long gone. We live in the Old Vicarage, next to the church.'

'My God,' I said, 'I know that house.' It was a huge rambling Victorian building with extensive gardens, down a gravel track lined with trees. Or, it had been when I had last seen it about 60 years previously.

'Well, that's amazing,' Liz said and then asked: 'Whereabouts did you live in St Neots?'

'Avenue Road.'

'So there is another coincidence, not that I believe in coincidences as I have the understanding that everything is meant, and has a pattern. What number Avenue Road?'

I had to think for a bit, and then it came to me. '69.'

'My daughter lives at 63 Avenue Road,' said Liz evenly. It was clear she was not believing what she was hearing, that this person, who had been a complete stranger to her not two minutes ago, now had not one, but two things in common.

'This is the oddest thing ever,' I said. 'First of all you live at Great Staughton. And now you tell me that your daughter lives next door but one, more or less, to my mother's old house.' Once again, I knew the detached 1920s house well as I had known the people who lived there in the 1960s. 'Avenue Road used to be the smartest address in St Neots,' I told Liz. 'Everybody aspired to live there.'

'It still is,' she said. 'It is the most expensive street in the town.'

'Why does your daughter live in St Neots?' I asked, as my memories were of a place where nobody would want to live if they had a choice.

'Mary and her husband are doctors,' Liz informed me, 'and not only is St Neots handy for their hospitals in Cambridge, but even though houses in Avenue Road are expensive for St Neots, they are still about half the price of equivalent Cambridge ones. She does tell me that there is absolutely nothing to do in St Neots, though.'

'It hasn't changed in that respect, then,' I said. 'There was nothing to do when I lived there. It was the town where nothing ever happened.' Liz laughed as I told her that St Neots had recently been named as one of the ten worst places to live in the country, full of yobs and chavs.

'I don't think that Mary and Mike are yobs or chavs,' Liz said. 'But I know what you mean.'

My ex-husband was also staying at the retreat centre and so I told him my news. 'You'll never believe this,' I said when we next met up, 'but not only does Liz Edmunds live in Great Staughton, near St Neots, but her daughter lives next door but one to my mother's old house in Avenue Road.'

Like Liz, Neville believes there is significance in everything and that there is no such thing as a chance occurrence. He also remembered my mother's house in Avenue Road and had his own recollections of St Neots as an idyllic spot, with its winding river, weeping willows and Georgian houses surrounding the market square. 'Not so idyllic if you actually lived there,' I had pointed out to him many times.

He had not heard of Great Staughton—well, few people would have done—but he had long been urging me to write down my memories of my childhood and youth. So far, I had not been able to bear to dredge them up into consciousness but perhaps now was the time.

Liz was quite excited at my revelations, thinking we must be sisters under the skin. We had the same first name, after all, and how often do you travel 5000 miles to meet somebody from practically next door? Clearly, our acquaintanceship was fated to go further.

So next time we bumped into each other at the retreat, she issued an invitation. 'You must come and visit when you are back in England. My husband Richard would love to meet you and I'm sure we must know some of the same people.'

'That would be fantastic. As it happens, I am booked to give a talk to my old school so perhaps I can combine the two visits,' I said. I told her when the date was. She reckoned that would be perfect for her and said that I could stay at her house, as there were plenty of now non-occupied bedrooms.

Liz Edmunds and I, about the same age, became friends for the rest of the retreat, held at the Rajasthan headquarters of the Brahma Kumaris, a Hindu-based spiritual movement run, unusually, by women, as most Indian spiritual groups are headed by men. Liz told me that she and her husband were members of The School of Economic Science and here again I surprised her as I knew all about it. Despite its name it is a spiritual organization, founded in 1959 by Leon McLaren who had adopted many of the teachings of Maharishi Mahesh Yogi. The Maharishi, of course, had become famous as the Beatles' guru, when they travelled to India in 1968 to take part in a Transcendental Meditation experience, and the teachings made such an impact on George Harrison that he was thereafter known as 'the spiritual Beatle.'

I had previously done some research into the somewhat controversial beliefs of The School of Economic Science for a book I had written on Eastern spiritual movements that had become popular in the West. Liz said that she and her husband had been spiritual seekers and meditators for many years.

I had come to India mainly to promote my new book, A Century of Service, an appreciation of the work of Dadi Janki, the now 100-year-old spiritual leader who started the first Brahma Kumaris centre outside India. Much of my stay would be occupied by giving talks and presentations and here I have to say that book launches are very different in India from those in the UK, where you are lucky to get half a dozen people to turn up and of those, perhaps one or two will buy a copy of the book.

Together, my ex-husband, promoting his own book, and I, filled stadiums and sold hundreds of copies. The talks we gave at various venues were packed, and there were always lots of questions at the end. It was extremely difficult to extricate oneself from each event as we were waylaid all the way to the car waiting to take us back to where we were staying. The only thing different from a UK book tour was that there was no alcohol at any of these presentations. In the UK, you wouldn't get anybody to come along at all unless wine was on offer.

But all the while I was giving the talks and travelling around India, I could not get 'Great Staughton' out of my head. Something shifted in my brain and memories that had been buried for decades were now rising, somewhat uncomfortably, to the surface. Great Staughton, an unremarkable village in itself, also occupied my thoughts while I was supposed to be deep in meditation.

It was one of the little villages where, in the early 1950s, my mother had set up an agency at the Post Office for her St Neots flower shop. In those days, few people had cars and hardly anybody was on the telephone, so it made sense for the villagers to order their funeral wreaths and wedding bouquets at the Post Office, from where they could be telephoned to the shop and delivered to their address. The setting up of village agencies was one of the bright ideas dreamed up by my mother's boss John Wingate, who had bought a market garden and flower shop after the Second World War. I often used to drive to Great Staughton with my mother and got to know many of the villagers there although I had no recollections of the Edmunds family. I knew the house because my mother had often decorated the nearby church for weddings and other events.

It had been more than 60 years since I last visited the village and I had not been to St Neots in recent years either, but a couple of months after the retreat ended, I drove down from Oxford where I was now living and reacquainted myself with the area. It had greatly altered, and many once familiar landmarks were missing, making it difficult to get my bearings. The Samuel Jones paper mill, for instance, had become a block of flats. St Neots itself, a tiny town in my day, was now surrounded by vast housing estates which had swallowed up many of the once separate little villages.

New roads and ring roads made it quite hard actually to find Great Staughton, even with my satnav, but I got there in the end to find the whole village more or less flooded. The former Post Office, at the entrance to the village, was now a private residence.

The propensity of the low-lying area to flood had not changed, then, and I remembered one of my university boyfriends remarking that the locality always seemed to be under water when he visited. 'That's the best place for it,' I told him.

Getting to the Old Vicarage was not so easy as the gravel path that led to the house was completely flooded and I was nervous of getting stuck in the mud. It was a terrain more suitable for Land Rovers than an elderly Polo being inexpertly manoeuvred by an elderly driver, but I just about made it. The house was a large comfortable farmhouse-style home, with a huge kitchen and a Labrador snoozing in a basket. Lots of muddy Wellington boots were just inside the door, and industrial-size tins and packets of food were in the larder. It was like a film set for a *Midsomer Murders* drama, and clearly the home of extremely affluent people, complete with authentic shabby-chic décor. It was not the home of people who had to buy their own furniture, in the immortal words of the consummate snob Alan Clark, as most of the pieces looked extremely old, as if handed down by former generations of Edmunds. There was a grand piano in the living room, covered in silver-framed family photos, and family portraits were on the walls. It was all very country-style upper-class.

Liz and her husband Richard, looking like a country squire in green sleeveless jerkin, check shirt and corduroy trousers—the uniform of the older rural dweller—met me in the kitchen and Liz, clearly the main talker of the couple, told me more about the house.

'Richard actually grew up here,' she said. 'It hasn't actually been a working vicarage for decades. And it wasn't a working vicarage when Richard's father bought it. Subsequent vicars have lived in modest three-bedroom semis in the village, although Great Staughton no longer has its own separate vicar. We are combined with Little Staughton and Hail Weston and of course, don't have services in the church every Sunday.'

'How did you come to live here?' I asked, as although the house was huge and the family seemed very wealthy, it was hard to imagine how one would acquire wealth in Great Staughton. 'We lived for most of our married life in London, where Richard worked in the City,' Liz said. 'Then when he retired, and Richard's stepmother moved out to live in a care home, we decided to come here and embrace village life. Richard's stepmother modernised the house to some extent and put up new curtains, but basically, it has remained the same as when Richard lived here as a boy.'

'Has village life worked out?' I asked.

'Oh yes. We arrange the annual fête and we have made a lot of friends here. I couldn't even imagine living in London now.' Their six children, Liz told me, had all attended a School of Economic Science boarding school, but had long grown up and left home, so Liz and Richard were rattling around in this huge house, just the two of them. Mary, the youngest, was the only one living nearby and the rest were scattered around the world.

Liz was a keen cook and had prepared a lovely vegetarian meal while Richard, her amiable 'mine host' husband, poured copious amounts of wine. We felt that there must be people we knew in common and on a whim, I asked whether they had come across Pauline Sismey, who had lived with her husband Oliver in a vast manor house in Offord Cluny, a nearby village on the other side of the A1 motorway.

'God, yes,' said Richard, starting slightly. 'I don't think Oliver knew what had hit him when he married her.'

'She was a friend of my mother,' I said. 'I often used to sit in her kitchen as they gossiped. Oliver Sismey was one of my referees for university. I always thought there was something strange about Pauline. Did you ever know anything about her background, or her son?'

'No,' said Richard as we sat round the scrubbed kitchen table getting to know each other. 'I never even knew she had a son. All I knew is that she was an eccentric woman who married this friend of my father. Oliver had been a bachelor, living alone for years after his divorce, and when he remarried, it was to Pauline. A most unlikely match, I would have said.'

'And yet it lasted, didn't it?' I asked.

'Yes, astonishingly. If you want to know more about Pauline and

Oliver, you should ask our friend Hugh Duberly, who lives just down the road. He knew them well, and also Prince Nicholas and Prince Yurka Galitzine, who were related to Pauline.'

Prince Nicholas Galitzine and Prince Yurka Galitzine; more names from the past. I vaguely remembered Prince Yurka coming into my mother's shop and knew he had something to do with Pauline, although I was not exactly sure of the connection.

'What about her being dumped in Paris as a child?' I asked. Yet another memory rose to the surface.

Once again, Richard did not know anything about that. 'We never delved into Pauline's history or background,' he said. 'I've no idea where she came from or how she managed to inveigle Oliver. She was this femme fatale type woman who came out of nowhere and established herself as Lady of the Manor.'

But my curiosity was aroused, even if Richard's wasn't. For the rest of the evening, we exchanged reminiscences about people we had both known, or known of. 'Did you know Bunty Redman?' I asked Richard. 'Virginia Walmisley-Dresser? Benita Bachelor?' More names from my past came up as it became clear that the Edmunds family had been part of the upper-class, or county Huntingdonshire set that my mother's customers moved in. After all this time, it was a surprise to me to come across somebody who had known so many people from my youth; people I had known before I escaped from St Neots forever.

Yes, he had known them all. Bunty Redman had been the attractive wife of Colonel Jack Redman of Waresley Park. 'Bunty and Benita Bachelor's mother were sisters,' Richard said, 'and Virginia now lives on the Isle of Wight. Virginia and Benita are best friends and Virginia often goes to her house to stay. She divorced her millionaire husband ages ago.' Benita, Richard told me, still lived in the house in Little Paxton where she had grown up and had turned it into a holiday resort. He said that Benita and her Irish husband Ninian would go to the Edmunds' for dinner once in a while. Little Paxton, yet another of the tiny villages near to St Neots, is about three miles from Great Staughton.

Isle of Wight? My artist friend Alex Williams lived there. He might know Virginia, whose family had also been part of the upper crust St Neots society and who had certainly known Pauline Sismey. 'My sister can put you in touch with Ann Walmisley-Dresser, Virginia's sister,' Richard said. 'That might help as well.' I was collecting lots of names from my distant past from Richard; now I would have to write about them. But the name that continued to intrigue me was that of Pauline Sismey, who was, unlike all the others, a woman of mystery.

These were just snatches, glimpses of gossip that I was getting, but I could sense that Richard was wary, knowing that I was a journalist and I think he worried that I might be planning an article, or maybe even a book, about these people. I did not tell him that I was considering writing about my early life, for publication, although he probably guessed. Liz whispered to me that if I was thinking of writing about any of the people we were talking about, Richard would want to know what I was going to say.

For he was a typical old-fashioned English gentleman rather than a rabble-rousing hack and would not take kindly to being quoted without permission. But he was right: I was now thinking about delving into my past, however painful, and these people had been a part of it. Somehow, they might all tie up.

I stayed overnight at the Edmunds' house and in the morning had a bath in the claw-footed tub that was huge and old-fashioned like the rest of the house, although Liz had made me very comfortable. When I went downstairs there was nobody there, but breakfast had been laid out for me.

There was a note from Liz saying that they had to go to Cambridge for a meeting, and she left me a box of six eggs 'from the Eggmunds' hatched by their own chickens. The note added that I didn't need to lock the door as their gardener was working outside and would be coming in for his cup of tea. I was slightly nonplussed, as I had not known they would be leaving early in the morning. I left them a present, a copy of my biography of the artist Alex Williams, who had also come from the area and who had been an early boyfriend, and drove into Buckden, on my way to give my talk. The roads were still flooded and I had to make several long detours, even to get to a village only two miles away. At Buckden, I stopped off at The George Hotel, an old coaching inn, for a coffee. While I was there, a fashion show was announced, and I was able to watch it.

This was organised by Anne Furbank, a former model who ran a very successful upmarket dress shop in the village. She was also one of the county set, or what was left of it by 2016, as she had married Richard Furbank, the son of a gentleman farmer who had lived in an ivy-clad manor house in Diddington, yet another of the tiny villages in the area. The Furbanks had also known the Sismeys. Perhaps I might get some information from them? There was no chance during the fashion show as the still glamorous Anne Furbank, now aged about 70, was one of the catwalk models. All of the models in the show were in their sixties or older, as was the audience. And the sudden interloper.

After that I drove through more floods to give my talk at Hinchingbrooke School in Huntingdon, housed in a castle and known as the most beautiful comprehensive in the country. This was not my actual old school, as that had been Huntingdon Grammar School, which went comprehensive in 1970 and had vastly expanded to its present size of around 1500 pupils.

After giving my talk on getting into journalism, and illustrating it with a photo of Philip Norman, the novelist and Beatles biographer who had started his illustrious career on the local paper, the *Hunts Post*, I drove back to Oxford, once again fording rivers caused by the torrential downpours of recent weeks.

All the way back, the name Pauline Sismey, Pauline Sismey, kept recurring and I resolved to find out just who she was as, years ago, there had been some dark hints about her past. Liz Edmunds had given me Hugh Duberly's email and once back home, I contacted him to see what he could tell me about Pauline, Prince Nicholas Galitzine and Prince Yurka Galitzine. Did he, for instance, know anything about Pauline's son? At this stage, I had no idea why I felt I had to investigate him, or if he even existed.

Rather like Richard Edmunds, Hugh was guarded in his response. 'I never heard anything about a son,' he replied. 'But I could never understand why Oliver Sismey, who was so staid and steady, had married a loose cannon like Pauline. I used to call her an old soak, although I have to admit that when sober, which was not often, she could be great fun.'

Prince Nicholas Galitzine, Hugh Duberly added, had died in his house in Great Staughton, and he also told me that he had visited Prince Yurka Galitzine and his wife at their lovely house near Stamford.

'Yurka had more luck than Nicholas, and more wives,' Hugh Duberly said. 'Thanks to his Russian, he worked for a time for the BBC's World Service, and he was also an artist.' And that was it. I could get no more out of Hugh, a former Lord Lieutenant of the county, even after sending him further emails with more questions. I think that Richard and Hugh, buttoned-up public school country types, sensed that I was prying, which of course I was. But I had divined that there were some secrets here and, like all good investigative journalists, I wanted to get to the bottom of them. I also felt that Richard and Hugh knew more than they were letting on, but I could not persuade either of them to be more forthcoming.

I resolved, for some reason as yet unknown to myself, to find out the truth of who, exactly, Pauline Sismey was. What would I discover? Would the quest be worth my while? I had a hunch that it would.

A mink coat of the type worn by Pauline Dennistoun-Sword, later Sismey

2

My mother's friend

S HE WAS ORIGINALLY known to us as Pauline Dennistoun-Sword and she was completely unlike anybody else I had ever met. Not, it has to be said, that I had met all that many people when, aged five, I first came across her, but even then, I sensed there was something different about her, something wild and untamed, perhaps.

She used to come into my mother's flower shop in St Neots wearing a short mink coat. It was more of a jacket, really, dark brown with vertical stripes, very silky-looking, with a swagger back as was popular in the 1940s. I could not take my eyes off that coat as I had never seen anything like it and certainly nobody else in St Neots had a coat remotely like it. She also drove a pale blue Morris Minor, in itself a rare event in the early 1950s as few women could drive and even fewer owned a car, although I could not be sure that Mrs Dennistoun-Sword actually owned the car.

Nor, it would seem, was she a very expert driver. She would annoy the other drivers by parking it anyhow on the market square, often taking up two or three spaces. It was much as if she owned the town and could park how she liked. She certainly had that air.

She was always heavily made up, with bright red lipstick, hair immaculately coiffed, loaded down with jewellery, and she trailed a cloud of Chanel No 5 or other expensive perfume in her wake. I particularly admired her long scarlet fingernails as although nail varnish was losing its 'fast' connotations, it was not in common use, at least not with the townswomen of St Neots, where all kinds of cosmetics tended to be frowned on as not being quite proper.

Standard St Neots women had hands and fingernails that not only did dishes but peeled potatoes, dug turnips, tackled the weekly washing by hand—no washing machines!—scrubbed floors and de-feathered and gutted chickens. One could not imagine Mrs Dennistoun-Sword doing any of those things as she was a fine lady. Or if not, she gave a passable imitation of being one.

The townswomen used to stare at her and ask each other: 'Who does she think she is?' The truth was, nobody knew. She was certainly very different from the squat, peasanty St Neots women as she was tall, reed-thin and indeed, looked very much like Vogue's Mrs Exeter, actually Margot Smyly, the supremely elegant 'older woman'—in her thirties at the time—and Mrs Dennistoun-Sword would have been about the same age, mid-thirties, I supposed. Not young but not old. She also spoke with a cut-glass English accent, which was, once again, very different from the broad Huntingdonshire brogue of the average St Neots woman.

And her name—Dennistoun-Sword. Even that was exotic and very definitely not a St Neots name. All this was unusual enough as most women in those days, immediately post war, looked plain and drab, not from choice particularly, but because they had no smart clothes to wear and mostly, could not afford regular trips to the hairdresser. But even if they could have afforded new outfits they were difficult to obtain as in the years immediately after the war many goods remained on ration, including clothes, for which a certain number of coupons were issued per person.

This being so, anybody who exuded even a tiny amount of glamour in those grey austere immediate postwar years seemed like a film star, somebody out of Hollywood or the pages of a glossy magazine. Such a sight was guaranteed to lift the spirits and even if people stared and tut-tutted, they were also slightly envious. But nobody stared harder than me, as a child already fascinated by fashion and make-up. I think I was too much in awe of Mrs Dennistoun-Sword actually to speak to her and I believe she totally ignored me, this watchful child taking everything in from the back of the shop. But the impression she made never left me, and the fur coat was definitely part of it. I used to refer to her to my mother as 'the lady in the short fur coat', as the coat made such a statement. At that time, I probably did not know it was mink, or even, what mink actually meant. I knew it was fur, though, and longed to stroke it, not that I would have dared. Like everybody else, I kept my distance.

One reason I remember the mink coat so well is that real fur coats were extremely rare in St Neots; well, they were completely unknown. Mrs Dennistoun-Sword was the only person in the town who had one. And to own a car AND a mink coat! No wonder everybody gawped at this strange woman.

She seemed bold and brassy, but the mink coat gave her some class. In her 1949 novel, *Love in a Cold Climate*, Nancy Mitford's monstrous comic creation, Lady Montdore, gives the following advice to her daughter Polly, who is about to come out as a débutante:

'The important thing, dear, is to have a really good fur coat. I mean, a proper, dark one.' To Lady Montdore, fur meant mink; she could not imagine any other kind, except sable, but that would be specified. 'Not only will it make the rest of your clothes look better than they are, but you really needn't bother too much about anything else as you never take it off.'

History does not record whether Pauline was a fan of Nancy Mitford, but whether or not she had read this advice, she certainly exemplified it. In those days a fur coat, especially mink, did not only make the rest of your clothes look better, it also made people slightly nervous of you.

And I cannot remember Pauline ever taking the mink coat off. It certainly frightened my mother's assistants who refused to serve her and scuttled into the back of the shop when they saw her approaching. 'I'm not serving her,' they would say and this meant my mother always had to serve her personally. Over the years, possibly because of this personal touch, an unlikely but quite close friendship developed.

When I first met her she was living at The Red House in Waresley, a village of about 200 inhabitants seven miles from St Neots. The other occupants of the house at the time, I learned, were her husband Colin Dennistoun-Sword and Prince Nicholas Galitzine, a somewhat swashbuckling figure who from his name was obviously Russian.

With such a domestic set-up, rumours swirled. Mrs Dennistoun-Sword looked a bit foreign: could she be a Russian princess herself? Another rumour was that she was a seductress who was always looking for a new man with whom to have an affair. 'Not that there is much choice in Waresley' went the gossip. But maybe further afield…

Her husband seemed to work in London during the week and as Pauline had nothing much to do, she had plenty of time to drive around in her Morris Minor looking for lovers. She certainly had no occupation of any kind, unless you counted chain-smoking, and rather like Princess Margaret, perhaps the greatest celebrity of the 1950s, she always smoked through a long cigarette holder. Very few women in St Neots smoked, although almost all of the men did, and that added to her fast-and-loose reputation.

One has to remember that in the St Neots of the time, a small East Anglian market town of around 5000 inhabitants, everybody knew everybody else and all about them as most families from high to low had lived in the area for decades if not centuries. Their children married the boy or girl next door or somebody they had met at church or, at best, a boy or girl from a neighbouring village. You didn't just know your neighbours, you knew their parents, their aunts and uncles, their bridesmaids, where they worked, how much they earned and whether there were any scandals or irregularities lurking in their past.

Thoughts and attitude in St Neots were at a level of conformity that would astonish today. And all this was in living memory; my living memory at least. There was, for instance, no such thing as homosexuality. Well, there was, possibly, and it was darkly hinted that one or two men who seemed somewhat effeminate were 'one of those' but if so, they were firmly in the closet and did their best to hide their orientation by getting married and having a family.

There was nobody of non-British ethnic origin in St Neots, either. There were no Jews, no Indians, no black people and in this staunchly Protestant area, even Catholics were considered odd and best avoided. There were quite a few Italians in nearby Bedford, who had been recruited from Southern Italy to work at the Marston Valley Brick Company, but they were derided as Eyeties and mainly shunned by 'respectable' people.

Furthermore, there was no art, no literature, no culture of any kind in the town and the most exciting social occasion was to have some relatives to Sunday tea. The men had their pubs and their sport of course but for the women, there was nothing, really, but to listen to *Woman's Hour* on the wireless and gossip to neighbours over the garden fence once the day's chores were done.

Nobody had a television until 1953, when a few families bought or rented one to watch the Coronation. True, there was a cinema in St Neots, but although film-goers loved the glamour of Hollywood and its stars, there was great suspicion of actual Americans, especially American men, or Yanks.

This was reinforced, perhaps, by the fact that there were several American air bases in the area and any girl who dared to step out with a Yank was considered extremely promiscuous. Later, in 1958, the scandal of the GI Brides made a sensational newspaper series that ran for weeks. So that, really, is how narrow St Neots was in the days when Pauline Dennistoun-Sword swept into town, and it took the influx of the London overspill in the early 1960s to start changing these entrenched attitudes; not that the overspill was exactly welcomed, either.

My mother, for instance, remarked: 'The overspill means that more people are coming into the town but they are not improving it in any way. They are all common Londoners, who will drag St Neots down.' In this, as it turned out, she was right.

Only one event had put the town on the international map and that was the birth of the St Neots Quads. Ann, Paul, Ernest and Michael were delivered by Dr Ernest Harrison on 25 November 1935 and were so tiny they were not expected to live. But as they continued to thrive, they became an absolute sensation, written up in the press worldwide. Dr Harrison himself also became world-famous. The quads were considered a true medical miracle and it is due to the tireless efforts of Dr Harrison and District Nurse Mailing—who with another nurse ran the Mailing and Daniels baby shop in Cambridge Street, St Neots—that they survived at all. Although known for ever as the St Neots Quads, their parents, Doris and Walter Miles, lived at Ferrars Avenue, a council estate in Eynesbury, next to St Neots.

Dr Harrison soon moved them into The Shrubbery, his St Neots medical practice, and oversaw their care. His daughter Winifred, who had qualified as an airline pilot, as one of the very first women to do so, used to fly milk for the quads from London, for the first few weeks of their life. Winifred was the first woman acrobatic pilot and from 1940 to 1945 was a flight captain in the RAF. She may actually have been one reason for Dr Harrison's experience in enabling the quads to live and thrive, as she was one of twins herself. This meant that Dr Harrison had already gained some expertise in multiple births.

One serious problem concerning the quads was that Mr Miles, a lorry driver, was only earning £3 a week; nowhere near enough to provide for his now five children, as the Mileses already had another son, two-year-old Gordon.

The local newspaper, the St Neots Advertiser, started a fund for the quads, and King George VI sent them £4 each, from the King's Bounty. But even in the 1930s, that sum did not go far and before long, the quads were sponsored by the baby food company Cow and Gate. Thanks to this, the family moved to a seven-bedroom house in New Street, St Neots, and people used to pay to come and look at them in their cots. As they grew up, the quads received so many clothes and outfits from well-wishers that they could not possibly wear them all and so they passed them on to other St Neots children of the same age.

One St Neots girl, Barbara Bennett, remembers being extremely well dressed in her childhood thanks to clothes being handed down by Ann, the only girl.

Doris and Walter Miles, who were basically simple, ordinary people who had never expected or courted world celebrity, did not want special treatment for their quads and they were sent to the St Neots County Primary School. They did not pass the eleven-plus and so continued at the school until age 15, as there were no secondary schools in St Neots at the time. I remember that Ann worked in Boots the chemist after leaving school but don't know what the boys did after National Service, which was then compulsory for young men.

I had just one encounter with them. I was about 17 and at the 21st birthday party of Sheilah Roper, the daughter of a local caterer. A couple of young men came up and introduced themselves as brothers.

I asked them, 'Which one of you is older?'

One of them replied, smiling slightly: 'We are the same age.'

'Oh,' I said. 'Are you twins?'

'Not exactly,' was the answer.

'If you're not twins, what are you?' I persisted, not guessing that they might be two of the quads.

They smiled at each other and then said: 'We are two of the St Neots Quads.' It was clear that they had been asked this question many times. 'Oh, are you?' I asked. 'You are the famous St Neots Quads!'

'We certainly are,' they replied. By this time, they were very used to being celebrities.

Even though I had not recognised them, they were world-famous. One of them—I can't now remember which—asked me out, and we went to the cinema and pub a couple of times together, but Paul—or Ernest or Michael—was much older than me and it all soon fizzled out. I never saw any of them again but at the time of writing, they are all still alive, now in their late eighties. They are the oldest quads in the world to have survived so long.

They were brought together by the *Daily Mirror* in 2015 to celebrate their 80th birthdays and at the time, had between them 13 children, 23 grandchildren and three great-grandchildren. Ann, as the eldest, or first born, was always known by the boys as 'the boss'.

Before their births, quads had only survived a few days, so they managed to put St Neots on the map in a way that nobody else had, either before or since.

3
My mother's shop

WHAT ON EARTH, everybody wondered, was Mrs Dennistoun-Sword doing in Waresley in the first place? Was she upper-class, middle-class, aristocratic or what? Everybody else in St Neots and around could be placed to within a millimetre of their social class. Of course, if she was Russian, that would explain everything, as somehow Russians were not looked down on in the way that most other races were.

The only Russians we knew, or had heard of, were the nobility who had fled the Russian Revolution. St Neots people were not generally well up in Russian history, but even they knew about Bolsheviks and Reds Under the Bed, as stories about them appeared in all the newspapers.

But before we get further into the story of Pauline Dennistoun-Sword, it might be useful to explain how she and my mother became friends as, even if nobody knew exactly what Pauline's background was, it was certainly going to be very different from my mother's.

From their first meeting in the mid to late 1940s, they stayed friends, becoming closer all the time. The link here is the flower shop. My mother came from a working-class background in St Neots and got a job in a florist's shop aged 14. For people of her class the thing was to get 'a job'; one could not be too fussy as to what kind of job and there were not a lot of options in St Neots.

Actually, my mother's life could have turned out differently, as she was offered the chance to train as a primary school teacher. But this would have meant staying on at school for another year, when she could become what was called a 'pupil teacher', a kind of apprenticeship to an older teacher who would show the young teacher the ropes. But as with so many families of the time, extra money was needed in the household as soon as possible, and it was thought that this extra year at school could not be afforded.

My mother's father, my grandfather John George Gray, who hailed from Southoe, a tiny one-street village three miles away, worked as a lorry driver for Linford's, a firm of local builders, and the family of four children lived in a rented three-bedroom cottage in Cambridge Street, St Neots. The house had no indoor sanitation, no electricity and there was just a cold tap in the kitchen, or scullery. My grandparents rented the house from Pibworths, a local builder, and because it was rented, completely refused to spend any money on modernization, preferring to live with candles and gas lamps rather than install electricity at their own expense. Needless to say, the owners of the terrace never spent any money themselves on improving the houses and just collected the rents.

From the start, it seemed that my mother had made the best choice to work in a florist's shop rather than to train as a teacher. She showed an early flair for working with flowers and before long, even a bit of ambition. Her brother George, her elder by eight years, had similarly left school at 14 and gone to work as a delivery boy for Barrett's, the local department store. He had soon started to better himself and began working for an insurance company in Stamford, a town about 30 miles away. As for Mum, she gradually worked her way up until she became a manager, moving around the country to bigger and better jobs.

'In those days,' she told me, 'the only way you could get a rise was to move to another job. Otherwise, you would stay at the same wage forever.' She was, although uneducated, intelligent, which was probably why she was offered the teacher training job, and she had a good business head. She had even worked in Harrods during the early part of the war.

But then she married, disastrously as it turned out. And everything started to go wrong. The first thing was that she became homeless. A lot of her tale of woe was, of course, the everyday story of people caught up in the Second World War, but my mother's somewhat soft-hearted nature was also to blame. She had married in 1939 and her husband, my father, was called up to serve in the RAF. She had met him when she was working in a shop in Aldershot and he had pursued her relentlessly. For a long time she gave him the cold shoulder, thinking he was not quite all there but in the end, aged 29, she succumbed, telling herself that his awfulness was because she kept refusing him. All too soon, she learned that it was deep-seated and could not be eradicated, whatever she did. He was liable to fly into unaccountable rages and with a face like thunder, not speak to anybody for days on end. She could hardly have had a worse husband but, in the way that things often work out, there proved to be some advantages in this misalliance for her.

In the early 1940s, my Uncle George's wife Florrie died of cancer, leaving two boys aged 11 and 13. Mother always found it difficult to say no; a little hardness of character would have served her well. George implored her to come and look after the boys Tony and David, and she readily gave up her job at Harrods to go to Stamford and care for them. In her favour, they all became very close and she was a kind of surrogate mother to them. This arrangement might have continued, except that before the year was out, George had married Edna, the hospital nurse who had looked after Florrie in her last illness.

When Edna came to live at the Stamford house, mother's services were no longer required and she had no choice but to return to live at her parents' house in St Neots. From early on, the marriage was a complete failure and Mum said to me later (which she probably should not have done, but she used me as a confidante), 'I used to pray that Dad would be killed in the war. But of course, as luck would have it, he was in Egypt, where there was not much fighting. Every time he was due to come home on leave, my temperature went up.' There was also some self-pity as she said to me once: 'I had no idea there were men like that. Your Grandad was so kind, so easy to live with and he always treated Grandmum with so much respect.' It was true that Grandad was the kindest of men, but at the age of 30, hardly an ingénue, she must have known that not all men were of the same stamp. But nothing was her fault; rather like Princess Diana much later, she always saw herself as an innocent victim.

For now, life looked grim indeed as not only was she homeless and penniless, she was married to a man who was showing signs of paranoia, jealousy, violence and rage, combined with low intelligence. And then, after five years of this ridiculous marriage, she became pregnant. I was born at home in the little cottage in Cambridge Street at the end of 1943. Mum was afraid that I would be born deformed or brain-injured with such a father, but 'when you looked like turning out alright, I decided to leave it at that, and have no more children.'

Unfortunately for all concerned that did not happen. When I was nine months old and still being breastfed—cheaper and easier than formula—she became pregnant again. In vain did she try to abort this baby she did not want for, as well as not having a home or any money, the tiny house was going to become ridiculously overcrowded. But none of the abortion methods—gin, hot baths—worked and in May 1945 she gave birth to my brother at Paxton Park Maternity home. Richard, as he was called, was a huge inert baby, weighing in at nearly ten pounds, and his birth provoked the jealous rage of my father, who was convinced the baby was not his.

Time, though, proved that the new addition was in fact his as Richard grew up to be a clone—slow, stupid, paranoid, jealous and soon exhibiting severe mental problems. 'Whereas you were always lively, crawling everywhere,' Mum told me, 'Richard would just stay where you plonked him.' When he started to move, and eventually to talk, he became insanely jealous of me, his older, cleverer sister, and hated me with such a grand passion that he never once spoke to me in any civil way. This intense hatred lasted all his life and was to seriously poison my mother's relationship with me.

I soon learned that my best bet was to ignore him as much as possible. We will look into his possible mental problems later as at the time, they were not understood and nor was there any therapy or treatment available that might have helped. 'Backward' children tended to be ignored and if there was one thing my brother hated, it was being ignored.

So now, stuck with two small children, one of whom was what was then known as educationally sub-normal, or ESN, living in her parents' house, married to a man she had come to despise and hate, she wondered whether there could be any kind of escape. The war was now over; my father had returned to live in St Neots, which made the little cottage even more crowded, with two small children and five adults, as my aunt Rita, crippled with spina bifida, also lived with them. It was all a heavy burden not just for my mother but for her elderly parents, now in their seventies.

And then—salvation! At just the right time, when Mum was at her very lowest ebb, John Wingate, a young naval officer who had been demobbed at the end of the war, came to her rescue. He bought a plant nursery in Little Paxton and a retail flower shop on the market square. The shop, called Paxton Park Nurseries, in gothic lettering, was situated between Barclays Bank and the Cross Keys Hotel, an old coaching inn. The shop was double-fronted and had several rooms out at the back where wreaths and other floral tributes were made up. Apart from flowers, the shop sold fruit and vegetables, seeds, garden produce, vases and containers and, what was very popular at the time, a huge array of cactus plants.

But before the business could get going, Johnny needed staff and he advertised in the local paper for a manager, called 'manageress' in those days. My mother applied for, and got, the job. After all she already had much managerial experience. She and Johnny Wingate hit it off right away, despite the difference in their ages and social class, and they began working together to make the new business a success.

So what about the two small children, me and my brother? What would have been a problem for many young mothers was neatly solved as there was a solution ready and waiting. My aunt Rita, unable to take a job or earn any kind of living, had endless patience with children and was pleased enough to have a role in life at last. Although suffering from spina bifida, in those days she could still walk and she walked the children for miles in the pram, as she too, wanted to escape the stifling atmosphere of the home. My grandparents were also pleased enough to help out with childcare and as it was, my grandparents' home became my main home for most of my childhood.

With my mother going out to work, full time or more than full time, I benefited greatly as well. The late comedy actor Roy Hudd once said that children who were brought up by their grandparents, as he was, were lucky and I agree with him. By living so much with my grandparents, I escaped many of the quarrels and rages that went on in my parents' house and also, it meant that I had substitute parents who were kind, stable and who, it has to be said, absolutely adored me. That adoration also caused my brother to lash out in jealous rages as, try as they might, they could not love him as much. He was just not lovable; this child who should never have been born.

Johnny Wingate was only 26 and had no previous business ex-perience, but by commanding submarines during the war, he was used to being in charge and he set out to make the shop and the accom-panying nursery a successful concern. He wanted to attract the county set, the gentlemen farmers and their wives, to his shop and here he had several advantages. He was young, ruggedly good-looking, upper-class, supremely self-confident and also, prescient. He foresaw that flowers, and in particular, flower arranging, would become a sign of culture and give the St Neots and District ladies of leisure something to do. Also, unlike many other goods at the time, flowers were not on ration and for those who could afford them, they greatly enhanced the home. Johnny was also a gifted amateur artist and designed a palette-shaped logo for the shop with the words: *The Artists in Flowers*.

By going out to work in 1946, my mother was not only unusual, but practically unique. It was standard in those days for women to give up their jobs on marriage and in many professions it was even a legal requirement. Men coming back from the war needed all the jobs going, it was thought, and women who had known some independence during the war years were shoved back into the home to become home-makers, financially dependent on a man and becoming, in the 1960s, 'the problem that had no name', according to early feminist Betty Friedan.

But it was not just law or custom that made women give up their jobs on marriage, as very often their husbands insisted on it. Here, my mother's marriage had its perhaps one and only good side in that her husband not only never opposed her becoming a wage earner, but even saved up threepenny bits to buy her a car. But higher class and more intelligent men did not want to be outshone by a mere woman and even when they married glamorous, high-profile women, expected them to be free to look after them and not pursue their own dreams. The book *Lives of the Wives*, chronicling five literary marriages, relates how Elizabeth Jane Howard relinquished her promising writing career to look after her demanding husband Kingsley Amis; how Elaine Dundy was expected to play second fiddle to her equally demanding husband Kenneth Tynan, and how Hollywood actress Patricia Neal was expected to keep house for her husband Roald Dahl, even while being the main breadwinner.

My father did not have the brains or the talent to make such demands and such was his low standing in my mother's estimation that she took absolutely no notice of him. By his very stupidity and incompetence at the most minor task, nothing could be left to him and he was treated as a child, albeit a very difficult one. In the early years, Richard did not present too much of a problem; that was to come later.

Being a housewife was so much not in my mother's DNA that I wonder now whether, unconsciously, she married somebody useless so that she could be in charge and feel superior. Well, just a thought, as it became the reality.

John Wingate had acquired the plant nursery and shop thanks to the intervention of a local solicitor, Guy Walmisley-Dresser, with whom he had been at the Royal Naval College Dartmouth. Guy already had extensive contacts among the local landowning class, as he and his business partner Michael Bevington, who together ran the St Neots firm of solicitors known as Wilkinson and Butler, did

John Wingate, my mother's boss and soulmate

most of their conveyancing. Guy and Michael also made sure they social-ised with their clients; Guy joining the local golf club and Michael joining their shooting parties. John Wingate, tall, handsome and extremely per-sonable, slotted easily into this milieu even though he was hardly a country boy, having been born in the Cornish seaside resort of Carbis Bay.

Guy's wife Sybil was already a friend of the Dennistoun-Swords and in 1949 their elder daughter Ann had won a prize at the annual Waresley flower and vegetable show on her pony, Tufty. The show, which attracted around 2000 people, was written up in the local paper in great detail and reported that Colin Dennistoun-Sword had organised the sideshows.

Guy and Sybil's younger daughter Virginia had vivid memories of Pauline Dennistoun-Sword: 'She was part of the crowd that my parents saw, and she often came to our house. I always found her scary. She was always heavily made up and had rather a ruddy face.'

Thanks to Johnny Wingate's networking skills, the county set from surrounding villages soon began flocking to the shop. Another reason why the business quickly became successful was petrol ration-ing. Until 1953, petrol was rationed for private cars but for some years after that, petrol stations regularly ran dry and customers were limited to so many gallons. If there was a high-end flower shop in St Neots, the posh ladies would no longer have to go to Bedford or Cambridge for their flowers and therefore they would need less petrol.

And then, the noble art of flower arranging was just getting going and my mother and John Wingate were in the vanguard of this new craze, now a huge worldwide industry. John Wingate had other ideas ahead of his time, such as establishing a launderette and a frozen food outlet, then both unknown on the High Street.

My mother, though, was not interested in these potential side-lines. Flowers were her thing and she preferred to concentrate on expanding that side of the business. And whereas John Wingate was keen on courting the rich landowners round about, Mum knew that the business also needed its tiddlers; the local customers who would come in for their packets of seeds, tomato fertiliser and pounds of potatoes. Her argument was that the leisured ladies would only come in once in a while for their exotic blooms whereas the townsfolk would come in daily for their fruit and veg—and the money from the tiddlers added up and kept the tills busy.

In the days before most people had fridges or freezers, the daily shop was essential.

Although my aunt Rita was mainly looking after me, I somehow also spent time in the shop, hanging around and in the way that small children do, quietly observing the customers. The 'posh' customers were by far the most interesting and I supposed I stared at them because they seemed to be of a different breed from the townswomen; more attractive, better-dressed, more confident, less downtrodden and certainly richer. Mainly, the rich local farmers married into each other's families and created dynasties which often went back for several generations.

With their children at boarding school and servants to do the housework, these wives had nothing whatever to do and had hours to spend fiddling around in the shop, matching up carnations, roses and the more exotic blooms which my mother bought from Zwetsloot's, the bulb and flower growing business that had been founded in the nearby village of Tempsford in 1932 by Dutchman Cornelius Zwetsloot. Naturally, being of Dutch origin, the company had originally special-ised in tulips but by 1950 it was a big concern and had many acres of flower fields and greenhouses.

Cornelius's six sons were recruited into the business and my mother became particularly friendly with one of them, Arthur. I can remember Arthur coming into the shop and also, going over to Zwet's, as they were known, with my mother. The older Zwetsloots had built themselves a large house they called Early Sunrise and there was also a modern bungalow called The Butterfly. Zwet's was strictly wholesale only, and the family refused to sell flowers directly to the public; thank goodness, as John Wingate and my mother would never have been able to build the business as they did if the grand local ladies had been able to drive their cars to Zwetsloot's and buy their flowers at wholesale prices.

For these women, usually with no money of their own and totally dependent on their husbands for their housekeeping or dress allowance, would often try to strike bargains and get a few pounds off their order, quietly annoying my mother when they were so much richer than she was. Zwetsloot's continued to expand and by the 1960s was one of the largest flower and bulb growers in the country. In 2023, it was still going, but had been renamed Flamingo Flowers, although some of the Zwetsloot descendants remain involved in the business.

My childhood, then, was very different from that of the other children in the town as not only did I have a working mother who went into the sumptuous country houses of the rich gentlemen farmers roundabout but also, thanks to her wages, we had more money coming into the household than most working-class families.

Sometimes, I went with her to these country houses which to me seemed like palaces with their huge kitchens, Agas, scrubbed pine tables and chintzy living rooms with draped interlined curtains, squashy sofas, a grand piano and antique furniture and piles of *Country Life* and *Horse and Hound* magazines. Their owners were gracious, and graciousness was a quality that was new to me. They were smiling, welcoming people as only those living in comfort and luxury can be.

I also had a mother who could drive, who owned a car and who hobnobbed with the local gentry, while not being one of them. St Neots people in those days were very keen that everybody knew their place and great scorn was poured on those who tried to get above themselves. 'I knew him when he didn't have two ha'pennies to rub together' was a common denigration for anybody who did manage to rise above their lowly origins. I remember one young man who came from a council estate and worked hard to qualify as a solicitor. Was he admired for making this by no means easy transition? He was not. Even after he set up his own practice, he was not accorded the same respect as, say, Guy Walmisley-Dresser and Michael Bevington, who were from the upper middle-class and thus considered to be more intelligent and trustworthy than somebody who came from a council house.

But all this meant that from an early age I was able to get a glimpse into something better, richer, more relaxed, than the poor terraced homes or council houses that most of the St Neots townsfolk lived in. My mother hankered after a council house and had her name down for one from the early 1940s. Usually such things would be left to the man of the house, but Dad did not have the brains even to do that. Actually, it wasn't so much that she wanted a council house as that there was no alternative. It was the only kind of accommodation that could be afforded at the time, and council houses were better appointed than most of the other rented houses in the town. Also, as they were subsidised, the rents were low, so there was huge competition for them.

Eventually, when I was three years old, Mum's name came to the top of the list and we were able to move from my grandparents' house to Cromwell Gardens, a small estate of social housing built around 1929. These houses had bathrooms, indoor toilets, electricity, front and back gardens and gas geysers for hot water. These were all great luxuries at the time but I already knew that life could offer more. And with the intense snobbery that prevailed in St Neots, people who did not live in council houses looked down on those who did.

My cousin Valerie, daughter of my father's sister Winnie, once remarked to my mother that only common people lived in council houses, to which my mother replied crossly: 'They are for people who haven't got much money, Valerie.'

But for my mother, now hobnobbing with the local gentry, the council house was just the next step and now, as a reasonably high-earning woman (for St Neots) she soon began to look around for something better. She began to save up to buy a house rather than rent one and Avenue Road was the favoured destination. The street was full of prosperous butchers, builders and shop owners. My grandfather's employers, Linford's the builders, lived in one of the biggest houses in Avenue Road.

It was very difficult for women to get mortgages in their own name in the 1950s but somehow, my mother managed to get a mortgage in her sole name from the council and so we moved into the detached, four-bedroom house in Avenue Road, where my mother stayed for the rest of her life. She had come up in the world as far as she felt she needed to. The house, if I remember rightly, cost about £3000 and she was able to pay off the mortgage in three years.

When she bought the house she told my father he could clear off if he wanted to but as it was he did not clear off.

Another cousin, David, Uncle George's younger son, who was always very close to my mother, said: 'He's too fond of his hotel life. He's too comfortable to want to move and try and find his own place. You will never get rid of him.' David was so right. He was a talented musician who became a lecturer at Sussex University and for many years, ran the Brighton Youth Orchestra. David was also gay and in later life celebrated one of the first civil partnerships. At Dad's funeral, he stumbled coming out of the church and said, 'It's grief.' We all laughed. David always hated my father and wished that Auntie Mabs, as he called my mother, would divorce him. But she never did.

From about 1946, when they led entirely separate lives, never sleeping in the same bedroom and rarely even speaking, Dad forged his own life in St Neots. Mum had got him a job as a driver with the Eastern Electricity Board and said that the only reason he kept it was because he was on his own all day and had nobody to quarrel or argue with. He became a special constable, refereed in local football and cricket matches and joined the Royal Air Forces Association, so had some cronies who regarded him as a 'character'. And then there was the pub, or pubs. Already he was on the way to becoming alcoholic and the only thing preventing him in these early years was lack of money. He was certainly not the kind of person I would have wanted as a father but I had little choice. My survival tactic was to ignore him as much as possible and treat my grandfather as my father.

Indeed, most of my mother's customers did not even know she had a husband and assumed she was a war widow, of whom there were quite a few in St Neots, and she did not enlighten them otherwise.

Another element of my life at the time was that John Wingate would often bring his easel, palette and brushes into the shop and paint the flower arrangements that my mother was making in the back. He would enter these paintings for competitions and those that did not win or were not sold were given to my mother, meaning that we lived in perhaps the only council house in St Neots that had real oil paintings on the walls. Paxton Park Nurseries was, at the time, the only aesthetically pleasing shop in the town, with its Constance Spry-type window displays, pedestals of flower arrangements and artistic pottery.

And so, as well as being introduced to the fine ladies who came into the shop, I was also introduced to art. As I had an early talent for drawing (which did not grow up with me) I studied John Wingate's paintings carefully. Oils and canvases were far too advanced for me at the time, but I loved to draw flowers in crayons and pastels. Art, flowers, fine ladies, some of them actually titled; it was a heady mix for a child caught up in it all.

At first it may have seemed that my mother and John Wingate had little in common. He was eleven years her junior, he had been to public school and Dartmouth and had been a Naval Officer and commanded submarines during the war, where a wrong or hasty order could result in many lives being lost. He also, at the age of 26, was married with two children. But yet they fell in love. Although never bold enough to divorce their unsatisfactory spouses and join forces, they enjoyed a clandestine love affair.

Once again, this was made possible by transport. Together, they would drive to the many little villages in Huntingdonshire establishing agencies with the local shops whereby floral orders could be transmitted to Paxton Park Nurseries. In this way the business expanded mightily and extremely quickly, and John Wingate also joined Interflora, a tele-graph service whereby flower orders could be made all over the world and also, be received from florists in other countries. In the early 1950s, to belong to Interflora was the equivalent of a Michelin star for res-taurants, and its slogan was: 'Only the best florists belong'. In itself the distinctive gold and black logo showing the god Mercury delivering a bunch of flowers drew customers to the shop.

How far their affair went in physical terms I have no idea but I have some snatches of their conversation which my mother, perhaps inappropriately, relayed to me. 'I said to him that before the war, I used to go to Portsmouth, where he was stationed, a lot, and he replied: "I was single then."'

On another occasion, when they were driving somewhere together, John Wingate said: 'I wish a man could have more than one wife.' My mother, knowing of course what he meant, said: 'How many do you want then, half a dozen?'

'No', he replied quietly, 'only two.' My mother always said that he was intensely loyal to his wife whom he had married, somewhat like my mother, in haste. There were so many of these hasty wartime mar-riages, often soon regretted. John Wingate's wife was Australian, but I have no memory of her. My mother said, 'I think her ancestors were transported,' although she had absolutely no knowledge of this.

Later, when John Wingate became a successful author, mother would buy all of his books and say: 'They sound as though they were written just for me. I can hear him speaking to me with every word he writes.'

They had the perfect excuse for working long hours at the shop and often being late home because in those days, funeral flowers were very popular and my mother would sometimes have to work late into the night to fulfil a huge order for wreaths, chaplets, hearts and other designs for a funeral in the morning. Sometimes, she would come to my grandparents' house where my brother and I were waiting, take us to our own house, put us to bed and then go back to the shop to work on the orders, with my father acting as babysitter.

The ideal in those days when it came to funerals was that the floral tributes should completely cover the raw grave. Nowadays, death notices often request no flowers but then it was a case of as many flowers as possible. Sometimes the shop would have an order for 50 or 100 wreaths and neither Johnny Wingate nor my mother would ever refuse an order, however impossible it might seem to fulfil them. Indeed, it often happened that the Paxton Park Nurseries van would be following the hearse, hardly managing to get all the wreaths made before the procession started.

I never minded my mother being out at work even though it seemed odd to my friends, none of whose mothers worked outside the home. I was happy enough at my grandparents' house, drawing, reading, writing. As a solitary although quite sociable child, I could always amuse myself. I did perceive, from an early age, that my mother's work, her career if you like, was far more important to her than her home life. She never created much of a home or home atmosphere but my grandparents more than made up for it.

As to John Wingate, I was very wary of him. In the way that small children often have but cannot put into words, I sensed that there was something special between him and my mother and I was afraid he would take her away from me. It was just a feeling, an intuition, and I wasn't sure that I liked him all that much. But as long as Mum was in his company, she was happy.

On the face of it, there did not seem to be much similarity between Pauline Dennistoun-Sword and my mother but something brought them together and kept Pauline coming to the shop. We did not very often see her husband, Colin Dennistoun-Sword, known as Sword according to Philip Norman, but when he came into the shop with her, it was noticeable that he walked with a pronounced limp, and sometimes with a stick, although he was not old but looked about the same age as she was.

Lieutenant-Colonel Oliver Sismey taking the parade at Offord Cluny, 1950s

4

Pauline scandalises the town

AFTER A FEW years of living in The Red House with her husband and the Russian prince, Pauline did something utterly outrageous. She ran off with another man. He was Lieutenant-Colonel Oliver Sismey, a divorcee who lived in his ancestral home, Offord Cluny Manor, a huge house with 15 acres of land that had been in his family for around 300 years. Offord Cluny was yet another of the little villages surrounding St Neots, about seven miles away and three miles from the county town of Huntingdon.

Oliver Sismey's friends were completely shocked and wondered how this glamorous, mysterious enchantress would fit into his very traditional lifestyle. Pauline and Oliver were quite elderly lovers by the time they ran away to London together as Pauline was then in her mid-forties and Oliver in his mid-fifties.

She quickly divorced her husband, the thoroughly decent mild-mannered Colin Dennistoun-Sword. Pauline and Oliver married in London in 1956 and, bold as brass, came back to live at Offord Cluny Manor and brave the gossip-mongers. She was considered a most unlikely partner for him and if she was deemed shocking before, with her mink coat, long red fingernails and scarlet lipstick,

Offord Cluny Manor , *seat of the Sismey family for 300 years*

she was now off the radar. Her elopement with the Colonel and subsequent remarriage was the most talked-about thing to happen in St Neots since—well, ever. And if the town of St Neots was shocked, then the quiet little village of Waresley was even more appalled, especially as Pauline's remarriage meant the end of The Red House and the departure of two of the villagers' most popular characters: Colin Dennistoun-Sword and Prince Nicholas Galitzine. Pauline had never been a particular favourite, and she was not even moving far away, whereas Colin and Prince Nicholas disappeared to live in London; not together though.

'I don't even think it's her first divorce,' said Margaret Minney, one of my mother's customers and another Waresleyite, when chatting in the shop. 'I'm told she had another divorce in 1939, and then she abandoned her son.'

'She has a son?' My mother asked in surprise, as Pauline had always seemed to her the most unmaternal of women.

'So they say. Never seen anything of him. One thing I do know, is that he's not Colin's son. Colin could never have children you know. Not after his war injuries.' The rumour was that Colin had been a prisoner of war of the Japanese, in Burma. But nobody knew whether this was true.

Now in her stride, Margaret went on: 'Mrs Sismey's mother is buried in Waresley churchyard, you know. She was Princess Elena Galitzine. And her grandmother's grave is there as well. But they're not Waresley people. They're incomers.' Miss Minney had lived in

Waresley all her life, in the same house, and remained naturally suspicious of incomers, as most of the villagers and their parents and grandparents had also lived in the village all their lives.

If Pauline was enigmatic and remote, Margaret Minney was just the opposite; completely straightforward and down to earth although once again, an eccentric character, not quite the norm. She was a spinster lady of a certain age, maybe in her forties, when I first met her, and a near neighbour of the Dennistoun-Swords.

Later, she appeared in a comic novel, *Slip on a Fat Lady*, by Philip Norman, as Miss Margaret Maxey (Minney, Maxey: geddit?) who is described thus: 'hideously ugly with a red gash for a mouth, like a wound, a square-face, a lantern jaw with cosmetics: the voice, gravel'.

The novel goes on:

Miss Maxey moved in front of the headlights. She was, to outward appearances, a man. She was dressed in tartan, a coat that shone enough to be velvet; a white shirt, bow tie and wellington boots turned down.

When Moorman, the hero, or anti-hero perhaps, of Philip's novel, asks his girlfriend Diana, once again a real person, Diana Harrison, and the granddaughter of Dr Ernest Harrison who had delivered the St Neots Quads and who lived in Gamlingay, a village next to Waresley, whether Miss Maxey is much of a character, Diana replies:

'Her father wanted a little boy and called her Jim until the day he died. She *says* anyway. The Dennison Swords [sic] who live opposite, are always complaining about the tricks her pigs get up to in the field. She's tougher than any man. And she doesn't like cooking and cleaning very much; once when she spring-cleaned her room, she discovered a little bird's skeleton under the bed.'

Not surprisingly, when this novel came out, Miss Minney recognised herself and was not at all happy. She threatened to sue the young novelist. Philip was terrified, but in the end it all passed over and he could

breathe easily again. He has since disowned this novel, later renamed
See Him Sweat, but it is a very lively, picaresque romp about a character
much like (one imagines) Philip himself, and the exuberant work of
a highly promising writer. Philip himself sweated when it came out
because not only does it caricature Miss Minney, but Diana, portrayed
as a sexy young tease, her German mother Ilse, complete with joke
German accent, Diana's stepfather Dr Tony Ellis and Dr Ellis's stately
home where they all lived, Merton Grange, in Gamlingay. 'How lucky
I was that they didn't sue,' he says now.

At the time the novel came out in 1970 Philip was already famous
as a star writer on the Sunday Times Magazine, but he had started his
journalistic career on the Hunts Post, the local weekly newspaper.
His mother lived at Southoe, a tiny village about three miles from
St Neots, with the gentleman farmer Gerald Davison, and they all
mixed in the same upper-crust farming circles. So Philip had known
Margaret Minney and one has to say that, however unkind, his portrait of her was accurate. Philip also says that Dr Tony Ellis, who was
a farmer as well as a doctor working at Huntingdon Hospital, was
deeply weird and 'almost as weird as my unofficial stepfather Gerald
Davison'. Philip also told me that his mother later acquired a fur coat
rather like Pauline Dennistoun-Sword's, wanting to be 'as good as her'.

Margaret Minney lived at Vicarage Farm and often came into the
shop with Pauline, as they were near neighbours. I can't remember her
buying any flowers or being remotely interested in flower arranging,
but she came in anyway, standing four-square in her boots and, like
Pauline, chain-smoking. She was the nearest one got in those days
to being transgender and although I doubt that she had any actual
surgery, she was certainly the most mannish woman I had ever seen;
yet another oddity from Waresley and she was what I suppose would
now be called gender fluid or non-binary.

As to her father wanting a boy, there is a story which gives Diana's
remarks some credence. Miss Minney was to feature in what was
perhaps one of the most highly investigated paranormal happenings
of the 20th century. It meant that, in psychic circles at least, Miss

Minney became famous, and she was written up, not just in a young man's fiction, but in a couple of serious non-fiction books as well.

The events happened ten years after Pauline had married Oliver Sismey and moved to Offord Cluny, but the two women stayed friends in spite of Pauline complaining about Miss Minney's pigs. They were, one might say, two oddballs living in a very traditional village who defied convention and lived life on their own terms. Odd characters have a way of seeking each other out, and with only 200 inhabitants in Waresley there was nowhere to hide. In an anonymous urban sprawl they would not have been so noticeable.

And then Miss Minney herself hit the headlines.

In the early 1960s, now living alone after her parents' deaths, she divided Vicarage Farm into two separate dwellings, one for herself and one to rent out. Her tenant was an Australian woman, Shirley Ross, who was interested in medieval churches, of which there are many in Hunts and Cambs. In 1965, Shirley had an Australian friend, Stella Herbert, to stay with her as a guest, and put her up in the spare bedroom. Stella had only been in the house for two or three days, when she saw an apparition one night.

In her own words:

I think I had been asleep for some time when I was awakened by a little boy kneeling at the side of my bed and looking at me with a pleading look. I can still see his face, so thin and drawn, and he gave me the impression that had he stood up he would have been tall and bony. His hair was fair and straight and falling to one side.

I sat up in bed, and although he did not speak I could feel he was asking me to call his mummy, and I tried to call 'Mummy!' The strange thing was that I knew Mrs Ross was sleeping in the next room, but I also knew that was where he wanted me to call his mother from. I could feel his hands clawing at my arm—almost hurting it. I can remember the sensation vividly. This seemed to go on for a long, long time and I was very distressed but not afraid.

Eventually I called 'Mummy!' rather loudly, and at that moment he disappeared. He seemed to be dressed in nightclothes (I got the feeling he was wearing pyjamas). Soon after that I went back to sleep.

Next day, when Shirley and Stella saw Margaret Minney, they told her about the sighting. Miss Minney went white and exclaimed: 'That was my brother Johnny, who died in that very room when he was five years old.'

Stella Herbert went back to Australia but Shirley Ross did not let the matter rest there and wrote to the Society for Psychical Research, who investigated the case, coming to Waresley to authenticate it if they could. Johnny's illness and death were corroborated by his nurse, a Mrs Kitty Hampton, who was then 95 years old but remembered Johnny's demise from tuberculosis very clearly. Any chicanery was ruled out, as neither of the Australian women had known about little Johnny and they hardly socialised with Miss Minney, since the rental apartment was completely separate. In any case, the women had nothing to gain from the sighting. Margaret Minney confirmed to the psychical researchers that she had never once mentioned her brother Johnny to her tenant Shirley Ross.

Later, the incident became part of a 13-part TV series on real or apparent paranormal happenings. One has to conclude that the Johnny Minney incident was genuine, in so far as Stella Herbert did seem to see the little boy, whereas most apparent such apparitions have been exposed as fakery. Margaret Minney's story is written up in *The Reality of the Paranormal*, by Arthur Ellison, a Professor of Engineering who became interested in psychic matters in later life. He wrote:

It is difficult to think of a normal explanation for what took place. The percipient had only recently arrived in England and had not been in the village long enough to hear about the death of a little boy in the house where she was staying. Miss Minney had never mentioned the subject to Mrs Ross and the only photograph of Johnnie, taken when he was three, was kept in a drawer and never seen by Mrs Ross. Critics who argue for 'coincidence' would have difficulty in accounting for the very distinctive appearance of the boy who had died there.

Johnny is buried in Waresley churchyard, with the just-readable words on the little headstone: 'In loving memory of John Alex, son of Alex and Florry May Minney, who died 21 August 1921 aged four years. "Until the day break".'

The early death of Johnny Minney, and the fact that her parents never had another child, may have prompted them to treat Margaret as their son and perhaps she wanted to prove to them that, rather like Enid Blyton's George, in the Famous Five books, that she 'was as good as a boy any day'. In 1937, Margaret had taken part in a local competition for women dressed up as men. It is not recorded whether she won but one can imagine her enthusiasm for this competition, and she dressed in men's clothes ever since.

Margaret Minney, top left, in a 'women dressed as men' competition. Waresley, 1937

In an interview with a relative trying to trace the Minney family as far back as he could, Margaret said that one of her jobs was to castrate the pigs at six or seven weeks old and also to cut the tails off the lambs. 'It was the only way of knowing how many lambs you had,' she explained, adding that the tails were skinned, then fried as food and were 'absolutely delicious'. Vicarage Farm was once a big concern, employing maids inside the house and farmworkers outside, although Margaret did say that the wages of these workers were very low and their diet was extremely poor.

My mother rather liked Miss Minney, who often came into the shop, always uncompromisingly dressed in men's clothes. You would have thought she actually was a man, apart from the slash of red lipstick, which always seemed completely incongruous and at odds with the rest of her appearance. In those days, women rarely wore trousers and Margaret made a striking contrast to Pauline, who always looked like a Hollywood film star.

Somewhat like Pauline, Margaret was an 'outsider' even though actually an 'insider' in Waresley terms and she did not fit easily into any recognizable known mould of male or female. She died on October 30, 1994, aged 87.

By the time that Pauline eloped with her Colonel, denuding Waresley of two of its most popular inhabitants, Colin Dennistoun-Sword and Prince Nicholas Galitzine, my mother's life had also changed. She never had Pauline's courage to get divorced, but it has to be remembered that before Pauline divorced Colin, she did have another potential husband ready and waiting, and one who had great standing in the locality. No, mother's life changed in quite a different way.

After a few years running Paxton Park Nurseries, John Wingate was called up again, this time to serve in the Korean War, in 1951. Because of this, he put the business up for sale and a new owner, a Mrs Bradshaw, bought it. My mother was by now too valuable to lose, and she was kept on as manager. The business moved its premises to the High Street, next to a barber's and with a flat above the shop. The Wingate years were over and I doubt that Mum ever got over the early loss of her friend, confidante, possibly lover and certainly—in her eyes at least—soul-mate.

Johnny Wingate never went back to market gardening and nor did he ever go back to St Neots. After returning from the Korean War, he became a schoolteacher, first at a preparatory school and then at the newly-founded Milton Abbey School near Blandford Forum in Dorset. He was not qualified as such, even though photographs of him at the school show him wearing an academic gown, and as my mother put it: 'He would have been far better than any of the teachers who did have degrees.' Never ever would she hear a bad or negative word against him.

At Milton Abbey, he began writing naval-based adventure stories with his hero, Submariner Sinclair, being a kind of naval equivalent to Capt W.E. Johns' air ace Biggles, and eventually he became a full-time, reasonably successful author. He wrote adult novels and non-fiction books about the war and in later life divided his time between Lewes in Sussex and France. He now fades from our story, although never far from my mother's mind. She continued to talk about him at every opportunity but after a few visits to St Neots on returning from Korea, he left his old life far behind.

But by the time he sold the market garden, my mother was well established as Florist to the Gentry, and the business continued to flourish. There were now agencies in at least a dozen villages round about and more were being added all the time.

She had four or five assistants and I remember the shop being a busy and pleasant place, with a good atmosphere between customers and staff. It was now an all-female concern and most of the customers were female, too.

The now Pauline Sismey started to rely ever more on my mother for friendship and solace, as divorcees, particularly female divorcees, tended to be shunned and avoided in the 1950s in St Neots. The upshot was that Mum would often go to Offord Cluny Manor and sit in the kitchen, the only room in the vast mansion that ever seemed to be used, and gossip over cups of tea and in Pauline's case, bottles of gin.

One day this former lady of leisure said to my mother: 'I'm going to start work.'

'Oh yes, what are you going to do?'

'I'm going to start a market garden, just like John Wingate.'

Although fond of Pauline, in an indulgent sort of way, mother knew just how much hard work was involved in running a nursery, growing crops and then selling them, and doubted that Pauline had it in her to establish such a business. She gave Pauline a wry smile.

'And,' Pauline added, 'you will be one of my first customers. No, don't laugh. I mean it. I shall be bringing you tons of beans, potatoes and other vegetables and you will have to buy them from me, not that chap from Cambridge', referring to a supplier who presently provided the shop with its fruit and veg.

After Pauline had gone, Mum said to her staff, 'That Pauline Sismey reckons she is going to grow vegetables and sell them. This is somebody who has never done a day's work in her life.' Of course, Mum did not know that; she only knew that as Mrs Dennistoun-Sword, Pauline had never done any paid or professional work. 'What does she know about market gardening?' She did not believe for a minute that Pauline would actually knuckle down to anything like the hard work it would take.

There, she was wrong.

My life had also changed. In 1955 I had passed the eleven-plus and now went to Huntingdon Grammar School, nine miles away on the bus. HGS was a small, co-ed school of only 300 pupils, drawn from all over the county and children who passed were considered extremely privileged as they were then able to have a first-class academic education, completely free. The school, built in 1938, had extensive grounds, tennis courts, football, cricket and hockey pitches, a library, science labs, cookery and woodwork rooms, a dining hall, assembly hall and teachers who were all university graduates.

It was very different from the St Neots Primary School I had previously attended, which had concrete playgrounds, outside toilets and no facilities of any kind. Being an HGS pupil gave me a new status among Mum's customers, although one of them said: 'They teach them sex at Huntingdon Grammar School and then they go into the woods and do it.' The grammar school had a small wood, or spinney, which went down to the river. Strictly speaking, the spinney was out of bounds and whether any bold couples defied the ban and went there to have sex, I have no idea. I suspect that, like much of the local gossip, it was just that, gossip, and had no substance in fact.

I was now being taught by qualified teachers, as many teachers at the primary school had no academic qualifications whatever, and I was learning Latin and French. Already, the first tentative steps of my eventual move away from St Neots had started and I thought that I would go to Girton, one of the two women's colleges at Cambridge University.

Although my home life was still problematic, I now had many outlets. I went to dancing lessons, ballet and tap; attended church three times on Sunday, mainly to escape the family rows that always seem to occur when both parents were at home, joined the church youth club and was mad keen on tennis. I joined the local library, got loads of books out and also read the books that my mother received every month from Foyles book club. Thus, I read through the middle-brow, housewife's choice authors of the day such as Naomi Jacob (another woman who looked exactly like a man and was known as Micki), Frances Parkinson Keyes, Georgette Heyer, Mazo de la Roche, the Chinese writer Han Suyin, Leslie Charteris, Nevil Shute, Nicholas Monserrat and, of course, Ian Fleming, whose James Bond novels were already making waves, and considered extremely outré.

Reading provided a great solace and escape and I also loved the magazines *Woman* and *Woman's Own* and vowed to be a magazine writer myself one day. Naturally, I kept this ambition to myself. And mainly, I was as quiet as I could be at home as I did not want to add to the anger and violence that were always threatening to erupt.

Richard, though, was by now becoming a serious problem. He was always at the bottom of the class, always picking fights with other boys and being rude to teachers. The teachers called his behaviour 'inexplicable' and wondered what was to be done with him, as he severely disrupted lessons, being a kind of class clown, except that nobody found him funny.

From being a passive, inert baby, he had turned into an aggressive, bad-tempered boy. Then one of the teachers, Bill Dawson, came up with a bright idea and suggested that Richard might take up rowing, as he was a strong swimmer and loved the water. It was a genius idea. Richard joined the St Neots Rowing Club and before long, his crew was winning cups at regattas all over the country. The house was soon so full of tarnished rowing cups that when he proudly bore home another one, my mother used to sigh and say, 'Not another cup to clean!' But she was glad that he had an outlet for his aggression and that rowing took up much of his time, as he had no other hobbies or interests. Here, at last, was something he was good at. I wish I could say that it was the answer and that as a result his temperament and behaviour improved. Alas, that was not the case. The discipline that was needed in rowing did not translate to other aspects of his life, but it required so much training that it just prevented him from turning into a juvenile delinquent, as my mother had feared.

There was another boy in the town, Robert Gregory, who exhibited similar anti-social behaviour and he ended up in prison, as Richard could have done. Looking back, I think that rowing saved him from becoming a criminal simply because the sport was so time-consuming and required not only discipline but being part of a team. There was no point in arguing if you had to pull together as one of an eight.

In later life, my mother would say again and again: 'Thank goodness for rowing. I don't know what I would have done with him otherwise. He would have ended up in Borstal.' Borstals were young offenders' institutions and it was considered a severe disgrace if your son was sent to one. 'You'll end up at Gaynes Hall' was a common threat by parents of disruptive boys, as this was a nearby Borstal and we often used to see the Borstal boys in their uniforms, in St Neots, being strictly supervised. We knew that they had committed crimes, otherwise they wouldn't be there, so we avoided them.

Today, there are schools for children with learning difficulties or special needs, but there was nothing in those days, and Richard just had to lump it at the local primary school along with the 30 or so other children in the class. As he was pretty much unteachable, at least by ordinary teachers, he was ignored as much as possible. It didn't help that, at primary school, he was in the same class as another Pauline, our Uncle Jack's daughter, and she was always at the top of the class. When Pauline went to Huntingdon Grammar School two years after me, she came top for every year that she was there.

Unfortunately, I was not friendly with Pauline as Uncle Jack and Aunt Doris, living next door to my grandparents, were not on speaking terms, proving that even in the most ordinary families, there were rifts and feuds which went back decades and never healed.

What was Richard's problem? Looking back, it is not easy to say, but whatever it was, it was deep-rooted and lasted for all of his life. Was he autistic or suffering from Asperger's? He was certainly on the spectrum as he could not connect with other people and had no empathy or moral judgment of any kind. He only ever talked about himself and took no interest in other people; a sure sign of autism. Some autistic children are very clever in their own way, being maths or chess geniuses for instance, but Richard was always slow and stupid. In later life, rather like Robert Gregory, he became a kind of Jack the Lad and was to cause my mother serious grief. I also think he was on the sociopathic spectrum as he had no empathy with other people whatever. No wonder that in later life, his wives soon ran away in horror.

With two slow, stupid and unpleasant males, who had no saving graces that I could make out, in my family, I wondered whether it might be wise ever to have children of my own, in case the taint was inherited. My mother used to complain that Dad, by his insane jealousy, had lost her all her friends, as they did not want to be in his company, and who could blame them? I always thought I had the worst father in the world and when, many years later, my schoolfriend Vicky complained about her own father, I said: 'At least he was in the normal range' and she replied: 'Only just.'

In those days, any domestic problems were kept firmly behind closed doors and we pretended, as far as we could, that everything was hunky-dory in our households. It was not until Erin Pizzey started the first refuge for abused women that these situations started to come out into the open and be discussed. Now, of course, it seems that everybody has mental health problems but during my childhood and adolescence, I thought I was the only one who had to keep the reality of my home life hidden. I could never, for instance, invite friends to my home as I never could trust my father or brother not to be rude, abusive, refuse to speak to them or show off embarrassingly in front of them.

But for all this, mother continued to work hard at the shop, always maintaining that it was 'her salvation' and the numbers of her posh customers kept increasing as word spread. Sometimes, a Prince Yurka Galitzine would come into the shop with Pauline, who would introduce him as her brother. Brother? It seemed that he was the son of Prince Nicholas Galitzine, formerly of The Red House, but I was certain that Prince Nicholas could not be Pauline's father as well, as this rather swashbuckling character, who spoke with a slight Russian accent, did not seem all that much older than her, and certainly not old enough to be her father. My mother used to say, 'Whatever sort of a name is Yurka?', wondering whether she had spelt it right when writing down his orders but she made no attempt to get to the bottom of the relationships.

Nobody seemed to know anything, and instead of having any curiosity, St Neots people just gossiped and spread rumours, never trying to discover the truth.

If ever I asked any questions, and I can't remember whether I did, I certainly did not get any answers. I suppose the grown-ups were a world away from me and in any case, children were taught not to be nosey.

As such, the mystery deepened and eventually, long after all the combatants had died, I felt I had to get to the bottom of it all. Nobody, so far as I knew, had ever investigated Pauline's background before. If I did so, what would I find?

5
Pauline's origins

THE STORY OF little Johnny Minney had intrigued me when I first read about it, possibly because I had known Margaret Minney as one of my mother's customers, so when I had the opportunity to visit Waresley many years later, I decided to visit the graveyard, to see what I might find among the headstones.

I had gone there with my school-friend Grahame Jackson, now living in Australia, who wanted to lay a plaque to his late father. As a child, Grahame had lived in The Grange, Waresley, a barn conversion designed and executed by his architect father and, as it happened, next door to The Red House, where Pauline, Colin Dennistoun-Sword and Prince Nicholas Galitzine had lived. The house, now renamed Water End House and no longer red, was joined to Waresley Grange by a huge two-acre lake.

Remembering now what Miss Minney had said years before, about Pauline's mother and grandmother being buried in Waresley churchyard, I looked around to see if I could find their graves. Most of the inscriptions on the headstones had long worn away and I could not find the Galitzine grave. But Colin Croot, a churchwarden, former head boy of my school and lifelong Waresley resident, had a map of the graves in the churchyard and showed me where the Galitzine grave was. The headstone had long toppled over and the grave had been neglected for decades but it was—just—possible to make out the lettering on the lichen-covered fallen headstone.

It read:

In loving memory of
ELENA EMMA LILIAN
GALITZIN
12 July 1886 — 20 October 1948

Her beloved husband
NICHOLAS GALITZINE
2 July 1889 — 6 April 1963

And her mother
MARGARET FAWCETT
HODGSON
23 December 1863 — 26 February 1945

These dates did not quite tally with those on the Find-A-Grave website, which researches the graves of Russian émigrés. There, the birth date given for Princess Elena was 1888 and that for Prince Nicholas, 1899, which would have made him ten years younger than his wife.

But I now had something to go on, as it became possible to trace Pauline's mother, Elena Galitzine, back to her birth family. She had been born Emma Lilian Fawcett-Hodgson in Liverpool, daughter of John and Margaret Fawcett-Hodgson. Her father's profession was given as fruit merchant. Emma had trained as a stenographer, a kind of early typist, and one of the first white collar jobs to give a professional salary and some independence to women. After her husband's death Margaret Fawcett-Hodgson had run a boarding house in Liverpool.

In 1911, Emma Lilian Hodgson, aged 22, was living at 7 Glenalmond Road, Egremont, Wallasey, Cheshire, with her mother Margaret Hodgson, née Parrington, aged 47 and a widow. Emma's parents had married in 1884 and Emma was born four years later. She had one older brother.

Once I had this information, I ordered the birth certificate for Emma Lilian Fawcett-Hodgson and found that these details were correct. Another entry on the Ancestry website ('a marvellous piece of software' according to Grahame Jackson, who used it to trace his own family's history) stated that Emma had married a Henry Suson Turner in 1914 in Manchester and then, in 1918, had married Prince Nicholas Galitzine, a young officer who was working at the Russian Embassy in London. This same entry also said that a daughter, Pauline Vincent, had been born to Henry and Emma Turner in 1914.

But try as I might, I could not find any information about Henry Suson Turner. The date of the first marriage, and that of the second just four years later, may have pointed to the fact that Henry Turner had been called up and was killed in the First World War. Clearly that was a distinct possibility, but no records or certificates of any kind could be found. There was no marriage certificate, no death certificate and also, no birth certificate for Pauline Vincent Turner, the daughter of this supposed union. I did remember that Pauline's second name was Vincent, as she often signed herself thus when writing cheques to the flower shop, so this daughter must be 'our' Pauline.

In spite of the apparent lack of records, two things were abundantly clear: one was that Pauline Turner, later Dennistoun-Sword and later still, Sismey, must have been born and two, that she must have had a father. Whoever he might have been, he had certainly managed to cover his tracks so effectively that he could not be traced by any search engines yet available.

If the year for Pauline's birth and the date for Prince Nicholas's birth were correct, he could not have been her father as he would only have been 14 years old at the time. Although this might theoretically have been biologically possible, it would have been extremely unlikely. In any case, another record pointed to Pauline's birth having occurred on 17 March 1912, which would have made Nicholas only 12 years old; a total impossibility. So he must have been Pauline's stepfather.

This seemed to rule out any direct Russian ancestry for Pauline, much as she had hinted to my mother about her exotic Russian

Portrait of Emma Fawcett-Hodgson, later Princess Elena Galitzine. Date unknown.

origins. 'I was dumped in France' she had said, 'where my Russian ancestors went after the Russian revolution.'

What appeared certain was that Princess Elena Galitzine, or Emma Fawcett-Hodgson, was Pauline's mother; and I now knew that she was definitely not of Russian origin.

Given that Henry Suson Turner could not be traced, and there was no marriage certificate in existence, I thought that the mystery must have started farther back than with Pauline and actually began with her mother. Perhaps Pauline was illegitimate and that was why an earlier marriage had been invented. But with no traceable birth certificate, it was difficult to know the truth.

However, it was possible to find evidence of Emma's marriage to Prince Nicholas Galitzine. Their certificate stated that they had married on 17 March 1918, at the Parish Church of St Mark, Hamilton Terrace, London.

Here are the details as recorded on the marriage certificate:

Bride's name: Emma Lilian Hodgson Turner, Spinster.

Groom's name: Nicholas Galitzin, bachelor, Prince, Russian Officer

Date: 17 March 1918

Residence of Bride: 17 Grove End Road

Residence of Groom: 42 Half Moon Street.

Father of groom: Alexander Galitzin, prince.

Father of bride: John Fawcett Hodgson, deceased, fruit merchant.

Age of bride: 29

Age of groom: 20

Witnesses to the wedding were Margaret Hodgson, Emma's mother, and also a T.H. Passmore and what read like Mary Vue Blunt (indecipherable).

This marriage was later solemnised at the Russian Orthodox Church in Welbeck Street, London. As a condition of the marriage, Emma had to convert to the Russian Orthodox faith and also change her name from Emma to Elena, to satisfy the very strict Russian nobility naming rules. She also, on her marriage, became a Russian subject.

There was another document, which certified that Nicholas's parents had given their consent for him to marry. Emma is also described on this document as a spinster.

Catherine Horwood-Barwise, Prince Yurka Galitzine's daughter from an extra-marital union with Clothilde Ward, said: 'According to my father, whom I never knew until I was adult, Nicholas had fallen head over heels in love with Emma and they married just three months after he arrived in London to work at the Russian Embassy as a junior officer.'

As it happened, Catherine had also been delving into Princess Elena Galitzine's antecedents and marital history, and we met up to compare notes. She asked: 'Why was Emma named as a spinster on two official documents when there was an apparent earlier marriage to a Mr Turner?'

She had also tried to track down Henry Suson Turner and a birth certificate for Pauline, once again without success.

The two marriage services, both taking place in church, also called into question a previous marriage for Elena/Emma. Until about the 1980s, divorcees were not allowed to remarry in church but could only contract a civil, or town hall, marriage. Clearly this would not be the case if one of the parties had been widowed, but if Emma had been widowed after a very short marriage, surely this would have appeared on her description? After all, there was no shame in being widowed.

There was, at this point, another possible explanation and that was that an earlier, very short, marriage had been annulled. In this case, it would have been as if the marriage had never existed and therefore, Emma could be considered a feme sole, or single woman. But usually there would be a court procedure to go through. Grounds for annulment were non-consummation, one of the parties already being married to somebody else (bigamy), or one of the parties disappearing without trace. Once again, no documentation could be found which annulled an earlier marriage. One might wonder at this point how Emma explained an existing six-year-old daughter to her new young husband, unless she didn't, and Prince Nicholas only found out later.

The address given for Emma is also interesting as Grove End Road in London NW8 was, and is, a very smart address. Where did the money come from for her to have such a valuable home at the age of 29 and being a stenographer and a spinster? Presumably the deceased fruit merchant father did not leave a vast fortune.

Catherine said: 'What has always puzzled me is where my grandmother's money came from. I discovered that in the 1920s she owned a property called Old Cheyne House in Tite Street, Chelsea, and when this was sold, they moved to St John's Wood, which was still a highly desirable address. That is where my father grew up.' Catherine added: 'The Galitzines always married for money!'

Perhaps Emma's smart address was an added attraction for the young prince. At any rate, three weeks after the wedding, the newlyweds went to America, where Nicholas had a temporary diplomatic assignment. On their way back to England they had to stop in Yokohama, Japan, as Elena was about to give birth to her only son, Yuri Nicholaevitch, born on 18 February 1919.

My memory of Pauline telling my mother, on several occasions, that she had been 'dumped' in France now had some ballast, as we had found online, under the name Pauline Turner, details of a naturalisation certificate dated January 1928, when Pauline would have been about 16. The online entry said that she had been naturalised from French to English, but when we tried to obtain further information were told that the document, held at the National Archives, Kew, was sealed until 2029.

Catherine said that she had never met Pauline and knew very little about her, but as a fluent French speaker, now tried to find a birth certificate through French ancestry websites. Once again, she

drew a complete blank, even though she had tried every name combination she could think of. She said: 'There are an amazing number
of Turners, Vincents, Hodgsons and even Fawcetts in France, which
surprised me.' However, none of the names fitted and the birth certificate remained untraceable.

This meant that a birth certificate did not appear to exist either
in France or the UK. Catherine now said: 'I wonder whether she had
been adopted?'

'If so' I replied, 'there would still be a birth certificate somewhere.
So far as I know, all births have to be registered by law and I'm sure
the same applies in France.'

'And then,' Catherine continued, 'why might a young single
woman adopt a child? And if Elena/Emma had already been married
and divorced, or maybe widowed, why would she be called a spinster
on two official documents? Another thought is that if Pauline had
been born in Paris, was she brought up there, possibly by another
family, only to return to the UK at the age of 16?'

'I actually think that is unlikely,' I said. 'If she had lived in France
for the first 16 years of her life, she would have had at least the traces
of a French accent, and that was not the case. She spoke with a perfect
cut-glass English accent. I also believe that if a baby is given French
nationality, this would have to mean that one or other of the parents
was French.'

'If Pauline's father was French, he had a very English name',
Catherine said. 'Vincent is perhaps more French, but I can get no
leads from either name.'

The French connection petered out but then I had the idea of
looking her up under the name Pauline Turner Galitzine. After all,
she might have taken her stepfather's surname, as is often the case.

Here my searches were more fruitful. Heathfield School came
up and there, online, were some of the old school magazines. In the
1928 issue of the magazine I found the name Pauline Golitsyn. Could
she be 'our' Pauline? Looking further, I found two more entries; one
announcing her marriage to a Reginald Daubeny in December 1931 and

a third saying that Mrs Daubeny, formerly Pauline Turner Galitzine, and Princess Alexandre Galitzine, formerly Helene O'Donnell, came to tea at the school in the summer of 1937.

So the rumours that Mrs Sismey had another husband before she married Colin Dennistoun-Sword were true. However, when I contacted the archivist for Heathfield School I was told that nobody of that name was listed as a pupil and the only name she could find was that of Helene O'Donnell. But although the archivist could find no records, she must have been a pupil there for her name to have been mentioned three times in the school magazine. The dates all fitted as well.

Catherine told me that 'Golitsyn' was actually a more accurate rendition of the Russian name but that Galitzine had become the main spelling, and Pauline's name was spelt both ways in the school magazine. 'The question now arises,' said Catherine, 'as to who paid her fees? My father was at Stowe School, which is also very expensive. So, where DID the money come from? I know that Nicholas never earned a huge salary and as far as I know, my grandmother never worked after her marriage.'

Heathfield is, and was, possibly the most exclusive girls' school in the country and very expensive (£36,000 a year boarding fees in 2023). It has also educated royalty, with Princess Alexandra being the very first British princess to have attended a boarding school. According to entries in the school magazine, Pauline was also a boarder.

After the Galitzines returned to London following the birth of their son Yuri, always known as Yurka, Nicholas began working as a journalist and artist. He also became a stage set designer, working with Cecil Beaton. There is a photograph of him posing with Baba, Cecil Beaton's sister. From the start, Nicholas had a theatrical bent and loved putting on plays and other entertainments. He was artistic, personable, good-looking and also, because of being Russian and a prince, welcomed into the highest social circles. A 1930s notice in *Tatler* magazine says: 'There is scarcely a social occasion at which Prince Nicholas is not present.'

He also worked for the BBC World Service, possibly thanks to his fluent Russian, and appeared to be a freelance operator getting any artistic and creative work he could find. It is doubtful that he made a large amount of money although he and Elena always lived high on the hog and at very upmarket London addresses.

In 1930, Pauline, by now naturalised as a British citizen, was presented at court. There is in existence a Pathé newsreel for 1930 débutantes, but it is impossible to tell which one might have been Pauline as in their white dresses they all looked exactly alike. She was now referred to as Miss Pauline Turner, so the surname Galitzine, by which she was known at Heathfield School, had been dropped. She would be 18, the usual débutante age.

Being presented at court, or to the King and Queen, was abolished in 1958 but until that time young ladies from extremely rich or well-connected homes would do 'the season' where, by holding or going to balls, they would hope to meet their future husbands, known as 'debs' delights'. 18 was then considered a perfectly acceptable marriageable age for a woman: Raine McCorquodale, 'three times a countess' and daughter of romantic novelist Barbara Cartland, married for the first time just a year after being presented at court; Frances Roche, Princess Diana's mother, was also married at 18, as was Diana Mitford, the future Lady Mosley. All of them were débutantes and much money had been lavished on their coming-out celebrations in the hope that they would soon find a rich husband and be off their parents' hands.

These very early marriages often did not last although frequently these debs married again and again. They had to marry as there was no way they would be able to earn their own living, not being trained for anything.

The idea that any of them might earn a living was never considered and nor, usually, were they given much education. It was common for aristocratic young men who had been to Eton or Harrow to go on to Oxford or Cambridge but any woman who went to university risked being denigrated as a bluestocking. It was considered detrimental to her marriage prospects if she was too highly educated.

At any rate, even though she had been expensively educated at Heathfield, Pauline did not go on to university or to any higher education and did the season instead. The deb of the year in 1930, the year that Pauline came out, was Margaret Whigham, later Mrs Sweeny and later still, the notorious Margaret, Duchess of Argyll, or 'the Marg of Arg' as she was known in the media. Margaret's father was vastly wealthy and her coming out ball was estimated to cost £40,000; a huge sum in 1930.

It cost a lot of money to bring out a daughter, as there had to be a different ball-gown for every ball, and then other outfits for Ascot, Henley, Lord's and all the other sporting events which collectively made up the season. Then there was transport to attend all the functions. Only rich young men, naturally, were considered eligible as they, or their families at least, also had to fork out for all the social occasions and 'at Homes' they had to attend.

So where did the money come from for Pauline to do the season after being expensively educated at Heathfield? You were supposed to come from an aristocratic family to be eligible for presentation at court and although Prince Nicholas might have satisfied the nobility requirement, even though he was 'only' a Russian prince, it is unlikely that he ever earned the kind of money needed to present his step-daughter at court.

Yet somebody must have provided the wherewithal to fund Pauline's presentation. Her coming-out was successful in that, the following year, aged 19, she married Reginald Daubeny.

6

The first husband

REGINALD, AGED 21 at the time of the marriage, was the son of a composer and music publisher who had also been a Colonel in the First World War. The family's name had originally been Donajowski, and was changed by deed poll to Daubeny, as an entry in *The London Gazette* confirms:

I REGINALD ERNEST DAUBENY, heretofore called and known by the name of
Reginald Ernest Karl Donajowski, of the Army and Navy Club, London, S.W. 1,
a Brevet Lieutenant-Colonel [Temporary Colonel] in His Majesty's Army, now
residing at 27, Lenton-avenue, The Park, in the city of Nottingham, hereby give
public notice, that on the eighteenth day of February, 1918, I formally and absolutely renounced, relinquished and abandoned the use of my said former names
of Karl Donajowski, and then assumed and adopted and determined thenceforth on all occasions whatsoever to use and subscribe the name of Reginald
Ernest Daubeny instead of the said name of Reginald Ernest Karl Donajowski
and I give further notice, that by a deed poll dated the 18th day of February,
1918, duly executed and attested and enrolled in the Central Office of the
Supreme Court, I formally and absolutely renounced and abandoned the said
names of Karl Donajowski, and declared that I had assumed and adopted and
intended thenceforth upon all occasions whatsoever to use and subscribe the
name of Reginald Ernest Daubeny instead of Reginald Ernest Karl Donajowski,
and so as to be at all times thereafter called, known and described by the name

of Reginald Ernest Daubeny exclusively. Dated the 18th day of February, 1918.
REGINALD ERNEST DAUBENY, late Reginald. 084 Ernest Karl Donajowski.

Under his original name, Donajowski had published E. *Donajowski's Miniature Scores*, which included symphonies, overtures, concertos and chamber music.

He later sold the music company and may have chosen the name Daubeny to sound more British, even though the surname was originally French. At any rate, by the time Pauline met her intended, the name Daubeny was firmly established. Pauline was marrying into a high-achieving, cultured family and most probably met young Reginald when she was doing the rounds as a débutante.

The wedding took place on 25 October 1931 at the Parish Church of St George, Perry Hill, Vancouver Road, London SE23. The address of both bride and groom is given as 2 Vancouver Road, but this did not necessarily mean they had been living together, although they might have been. It was just a convenient address from which to get married.

The marriage certificate states that Reginald Daubeny is a bachelor and gives his profession as 'gentleman'. His father, Reginald Ernest Daubeny, is also described as a gentleman, and so is Pauline Vincent Turner's father, named on this certificate as Henry Stanley Turner, deceased. The Henry Suson Turner named on the Ancestry site as Princess Elena's first husband had transmogrified on this certificate as Henry Stanley Turner, conveniently dead by the time of the wedding.

Reginald Senior was a witness at this wedding, as was an H. Sutton Timmis.

Mr Timmis was a highly successful businessman and industrialist in Liverpool, closely connected to the Gossage family which became extremely rich through patenting a method of producing soap that lathered easily. The first Gossage had been a chemist. At this stage I had no idea what connection Mr Timmis might have to Pauline's family although of course Princess Elena/Emma had originally hailed from Liverpool.

What we do know is that the new 19-year-old Mrs Pauline Daubeny was a rich young woman. She and her husband moved into a large house where neither of them, so far as can be established, felt the need to do any work. Reginald dabbled in various business ventures including being a timber merchant but he only seemed to dabble, preferring the life of a man of leisure.

With most marriages of the time, children would soon appear, very often less than a year after the wedding. This did not happen, however, with the Daubenys, and it was only seven years later that their son John Henry Reginald came along, on 15 January 1938. Ah, so this must be the mysterious son that Pauline occasionally spoke about, but whom nobody had ever seen.

If this boy had been born in 1938, he would only have been about ten years old when Pauline first started coming into my mother's shop in her mink coat. But there had been no boy and nobody in Waresley had ever had any sighting of one.

At the time of his birth, the Daubenys were living at 21 Marlborough Place, St John's Wood. This was a detached house with four bedrooms, five bathrooms and four reception rooms. In 2020, it had a value of £9 million. On John Henry Reginald's birth certificate, his father's occupation is given as finance company director, which could of course mean anything.

Whatever the source of the finances, they did ensure that Pauline and Reginald were living at a sumptuous house at a highly desirable address; not bad for a 25-year-old woman and a 29-year-old man. Pauline's profession of course is not given. That of wife and mother was considered occupation enough, and even if the mother did follow a career, there was no space for its inclusion on the birth certificates of the day.

By the time John Henry Reginald was born or maybe even before, Pauline was tiring of her husband and had her eye on a dashing young aspiring barrister called John Colin Dennistoun-Sword. He was a noted sportsman who was an accomplished cricketer, playing for his school, and also an expert skier. In 1935, instead of going to university, he had been admitted to Lincoln's Inn, one of the four

Inns of Court. At the time he and Pauline met, he was aged 22 and she was four years older.

Pauline did not hesitate. When John Henry Reginald was just over a year old, she decided to divorce Reginald, and the Decree Nisi was issued on 21 April 1939 with Pauline named as the Petitioner and Reginald as the Respondent. On the divorce certificate Reginald had admitted to adultery although it was most probably Pauline who was the adulterous party as she was already carrying on an affair with Colin. It was the usual thing, at least in upper-class divorces of the time, for the husband to agree to be the guilty party, even if he was innocent, as in that way, he could protect his wife's reputation. At about the same time as Pauline was divorcing Reginald Daubeny, another upper-class divorce hit the headlines; that between Diana Mitford and her first husband Bryan Guinness. Diana was aged 22 at the time and had two small children. She left Bryan for Sir Oswald Mosley, openly becoming his mistress when he was still married with three small children. Bryan was named the guilty party in the divorce, and in her memoir *Wait For Me*, Diana's sister Debo Devonshire writes: 'Bryan went through the motions of spending a night with a prostitute in a Brighton hotel which in those days was how many divorces were arranged.'

There was usually a six-month gap between the Decree Nisi and the Decree Absolute being issued, during which time either party had a chance to show sufficient cause why the decree should not be made absolute and the marriage dissolved. In the Daubeny case there was no objection and the marriage solemnised on 25 October 1931 at St George's Church, Perry Hill, was officially and legally dissolved on 13 September 1939.

That very same day, Pauline married Colin Dennistoun-Sword at Aldershot, where he was now stationed, waiting to go to the war which had been declared on 1 September 1939.

But in the six months between the Decree Nisi and Pauline's second marriage to Colin Dennistoun-Sword, she was involved in some very dramatic happenings indeed. Her divorce and remarriage were perhaps the least astonishing of these events.

7

'A wealthy Russian princess'

A S IT HAPPENED 1939 was a momentous year for Pauline as not only did she divorce and remarry, she got her name into every newspaper of the day.

The first thing she did was to join The Right Club, a far-right organization that had been founded by Archibald Maude Ramsay, a British Army Officer who later became a Scottish Union MP. Colin Dennistoun-Sword and Prince Yurka Galitzine, then aged 20, also joined. During the late 1930s, Ramsay became increasingly convinced that Jews were at the heart of Communism and that Britain needed to be rid of British Jewry. Ramsay came to believe that even the British Conservative Party was under Jewish control and the Right Club had the avowed aim of freeing Britain from 'Jewish malevolence'. The Club was founded to link up both those who opposed Jews and the seemingly inevitable coming war with Germany.

Ramsay believed there was a Jewish plot to take over the world and that Jews had to be opposed by any means possible. He soon attracted leading British Fascists to the Club: Oswald Mosley and Lord Redesdale ('Uncle Matthew' in Nancy Mitford's The Pursuit of Love) both became members. Lord Redesdale's daughter Diana had married Mosley immediately after her divorce from Bryan Guinness, in Nazi propaganda Minister Joseph Goebbels' drawing room in October 1936.

From the start the Right Club attracted the upper classes and British aristocracy who were terrified that Communism would take over the country and take away their privileges. They remembered the Russian Revolution, where the royal family was murdered by communists and members of the nobility had to flee. There is no suggestion, though, that Prince Nicholas Galitzine was involved in the Right Club. In a book published in 2021, *Nazis and Nobles*, author Stephen Malinowski says that Hitler himself courted the German nobility with the same aim of ridding the country of Jewish influence and establishing the pure Aryan race. There was also in Britain at the time, and possibly in Germany as well, a great fear that if Communism came in and equalised everybody, the upper classes would no longer have the lower orders working for them on starvation wages.

It was a prospect that, for those who had enjoyed often unearned and undeserved privileges going back centuries, could not be contemplated.

It is not clear what attracted Pauline, Colin Dennistoun-Sword and young Yurka to the club but maybe they too genuinely believed that Communism was an evil that had to be fought by any means possible. The club met at the Russian tea rooms of Anna Wolkoff, a fashion designer who was also a Russian émigrée and staunchly anti-Semitic herself. Anna was a White Russian, the daughter of an Imperial Russian navy admiral who had been reduced to running a London teashop. Members were listed in a book known as *The Red Book*, which was seized by the Special Branch in 1940, after which the Club was disbanded. Anna Wolkoff was sent to prison as a spy. Unknown to members, MI5 agents had infiltrated the Club right from the start and the British government was kept fully informed of all its activities. In 1939, some members had been arrested and the Club was in any case a spent force by mid-1940, after the Second World War had started. Ramsay was also arrested and imprisoned.

The full list of Right Club members was kept secret until July 2010 when author Robin Saikia got hold of a copy and published a complete list of those involved. He said:

Yurka Galitzine was one of the young and naïve army officers who was attracted by the cloak and dagger activities of the Right Club.

Yurka appears with his future brother-in-law Colin Dennistoun-Sword, a lieutenant in the Gordon Highlanders. Colin's future wife was Pauline Daubeny, also a Right Club member.

Author Len Deighton, who was eleven years old at the time, lived with his parents next door to Anna Wolkoff, and Deighton's mother worked as her cook. Deighton credits this connection with the start of his fascination with the spy world and as the later author of highly successful spy novels. He writes in *The Deighton Dossier*:

Anna Wolkoff was the 38-year-old daughter of a one-time admiral of the Imperial Russian Navy. He had been the Russian Embassy's naval attaché until the revolution in 1917. Anna's mother had been a Maid of Honour to the Czarina. Granted political asylum, and naturalised, the Wolkoffs now had a 'Russian tearoom' opposite South Kensington Underground Railway Station. It was noted for its caviar and for serving lemon tea in glasses using a silver samovar. It was a gathering place for Russian expatriates whose bitter views of Lenin and Stalin had softened their feelings about Hitler and his Nazi regime. They were not all Russians. Members of the Right Club, a small organization of upper-class people with right-wing views, were also to be found there.

It was in early May 1940 that I heard cars arriving in the middle of the night. Crammed shoulder to shoulder with my parents, I leaned out of the window. There were two police cars in the mews and Special Branch officers were banging on Anna Wolkoff's door. They bundled her into a car to face charges of espionage. She was sentenced to ten years in prison.

Although Pauline's name as a member of the Right Club did not come to light until the full list of members was published in 2010, she became famous in another way in April and July 1939, just at the time her divorce from Reginald Daubeny was going through.

In April 1939, tabloid newspapers were full of the sensational news that the heir to the Marquess of Bristol, the Honourable Victor Hervey, aged 23, had been arrested for breaking and entering, and, with three accomplices, stealing jewellery and furs from two London addresses. The first charge was that the gang had, over the Easter weekend, stolen from Pauline Daubeny ten rings, a tie-pin, three brooches, two necklaces, six bracelets and a mink coat collectively valued at £2,500 (around £200,000 today). In his book *Playboys and Mayfair Men*, which gives a detailed account of the case, Angus McLaren says that Pauline Daubeny and her half-brother Prince Yurka Galitzine moved in the same social circles as Hervey.

George Hering, one of the accomplices, wrote a newspaper column under the name Peter Proud, and he had been at Stowe School at the same time as Yurka Galitzine. Possibly through Yurka, Hering got to hear that Pauline would be away in the country over Easter, and that her flat would be empty. It also seems that Hering, for some reason, had a key to the flat.

Having successfully plundered Pauline's property, the gang moved on to another heist and robbed another wealthy woman, Gabrielle Burley, of similar valuables. After the robbery, Hervey sent Pauline a bunch of flowers, although he did not offer to return the stolen goods.

It seems, from newspaper reports, that Pauline had now moved from the Marlborough Street house as her address was given as Queen Street, Mayfair. Presumably by this date she had already separated from Reginald Daubeny as the other occupant of the property was named as Prince Yurka Galitzine. In a *Daily Mail* report for 22 April 1939, Pauline Daubeny was described as 'the twenty-six-year-old daughter of the White Russian Princess Nicholas Galitzine, who was in the midst of divorcing her husband Reginald Daubeny.'

The case came to the Old Bailey in July 1939 and a *Daily Mail* story pictures Pauline striding into court looking very imperious, wearing a hat and a lofty expression. She was described in the papers as 'a wealthy Russian princess' and 'a society beauty'. Hervey was found guilty of the robberies and sentenced to three years' penal servitude,

Daily Mirror report of the jewel and furs robbery, 7 July 1939

*Pauline Daubeny
arriving at the Old
Bailey, 4 July 1939*

a heavy sentence for an aristocrat but he served it with some grace. He was, however, completely unrepentant and regarded the robberies as just a bit of harmless fun, a naughty prank.

Although an aristocrat, Hervey was, perhaps, not quite the sort of person a loving father would wish his daughter to marry. He had been involved in theft and petty crime from an early age even though he did not need the money, and he became known as The Pink Panther of his day. He was associated with a gang of former public schoolboys known as The Mayfair Playboys, who had earlier assaulted and robbed a jeweller from Cartier whom they had tricked into going to a hotel with some jewellery for a possible sale. The jeweller was attacked and badly injured and for this crime, two of the gang, although not

Hervey, were sentenced to being flogged with the cat-o'nine tails; a punishment which horrified the nation and which resulted in this barbaric ordeal, usually carried out on sailors at sea, being brought to a timely end. It seems that Hervey was not personally involved in this particular robbery, although for the rest of his life he was associated with it.

But shameless to the last, he later sold an article to a newspaper about his life and exploits, including the thefts and his prison sentence. It was reported that Hervey's father, the 5th Marquess, broke down in tears on hearing the sentence that had been passed on his wayward son. Previously, the Herveys had been a highly respectable family, although notoriety was to follow them later when Hervey's daughters, Lady Victoria and Lady Isabella Hervey, from his third marriage to Yvonne Sutton, became infamous as 'it' girls and socialites.

In the appendix to his book, Angus McLaren notes that Reginald Daubeny, Pauline's first husband, was prosecuted during the war for talking about Operation Torch, the Anglo-American invasion of French Morocco and Algeria in 1942. He had also earlier, before the war, been fined for a motoring offence. Daubeny was cashiered and sentenced to twelve months' imprisonment for the war crime but thereafter, he seems to have gone straight.

As for Pauline, the momentous year that saw her become a member of the Right Club, written up as a wealthy Russian Princess and get divorced from Daubeny, came to a high on 13 September 1939 when she married John Colin Dennistoun-Sword at an Aldershot Register Office.

On the marriage certificate, Colin was described as being a bachelor, aged 23, and his address was given as Talavera Barracks, Aldershot. The Second World War had been declared on 1 September 1939 and Colin was now a Lieutenant with the Gordon Highlanders. His father was named as John Gow Dennistoun-Sword, of independent means. Actually he was a solicitor, still in practice.

Details for Pauline on the certificate are given as follows: she was aged 27 and described as Pauline Vincent Daubeny, formerly Turner and her 'condition' as being formerly the wife of Reginald Ernest John

Daubeny, from whom she obtained a divorce. No 'rank or profession' was given and her address on the certificate was listed as 28 Elm Tree Road, London NW6.

This means that the Queen Street flat must have been a temporary address. Once again, her father on the certificate is named as Henry Stanley Turner, deceased, and his rank or profession as being of independent means. The two witnesses at this wedding were Zoe Ramsay, Colin's sister (no relation of the Right Club Ramsay) and B.A. Brooke. Captain B.A. Brooke was a close friend of Colin's and a second lieutenant in the 1st Battalion of the Gordon Highlanders.

Possibly because of the court case and wide publicity given to it, with Pauline Daubeny temporarily becoming a celebrity, her second wedding merited a newspaper report. I came across it in the *Cambridge Daily News*, although it may have appeared in other papers as well.

Under the headline, Mrs Daubeny Weds Again, with the subhead Daughter of Princess, the news report reads:

Mrs Pauline Daubeny, who gave evidence at the Old Bailey Trial of four Mayfair men who were sentenced for stealing jewellery worth £5,360, was married at Aldershot on September 13th to Mr Colin Dennistoun-Sword, only son of Mr and Mrs J.G. Dennistoun-Sword of Glottenham, Robertsbridge, it is announced today.

The only daughter of Princess Nicholas Galitzine and the late Mr H.S. Turner, Mrs Daubeny, as Miss Pauline Turner, was presented at court in 1930. She is a keen sportswoman and a clever linguist. She was married in 1931 to Mr Reginald E.J. Daubeny 3rd Carabiniers (Prince of Wales' Dragoon Guards) the only son of Colonel R.E. Daubeny. The marriage was dissolved earlier this year.

Jewellery worth £2,500 was stolen from Mrs Daubeny's flat in Queen Street, Mayfair, last Easter, while she was spending the weekend in the country. In connection with the robbery, the four were sentenced to imprisonment at the Old Bailey.

In none of the media reports were any questions asked about

where Mrs Daubeny's valuable stack of jewellery came from. Nor, as would happen today, was there an 'exclusive' interview with her, which would have made good reading. If the robbery had occurred in 2023, Pauline would have been asked to write a book about her 'wealthy Russian' origins, the robbery and her subsequent remarriage. She would have become a celebrity, a personality and she certainly had the looks and manner to carry it off. It was all juicy tabloid fodder or would have been at a later date. As it was, the story never received the saturation coverage it would have done subsequently but perhaps in 1939 the nation had other things on its mind.

So far as the jewellery and fur coat were concerned, Pauline did eventually recover the goods and the mink coat was the same one that she wore in St Neots in the late 1940s and early 50s. It was perhaps assumed that as a 'wealthy Russian princess' she had inherited the jewellery from her noble ancestors.

Also, nowhere in any of the stories is there any mention of Pauline being the mother of a young son. In the census of October 1939, her address is given as 28 Elm Tree Road, which is where Princess Elena and Prince Nicholas Galitzine lived. Elm Tree Road was known as an expensive, upmarket street where many artists and creative people lived. The Road housed so many famous people that it now has its own website and for number 28, there is this entry:

In No 28, 42-year-old Prince Nicholas Galitzine, journalist and artist, was with his wife Elena and Pauline Dennistoun Sword aged 27, all living on private means, plus a parlour maid.

The census was carried out in October 1939, and Pauline was living there because just two weeks after her marriage, Colin was called up to serve in the war with the 1st Battalion Gordon Highlanders.

In 2014, 28 Elm Tree Road was sold for £17 million. But at the end of 1939, the three of them were not to live there for much longer. At some time in the 1930s, Princess Elena Galitzine had bought The Red House in Waresley, where they lived for part of the year. It is not known exactly why they came to Waresley but their attention might have been alerted when the whole of the village came up for auction in 1932. Previously it had been owned by one family, the Duncombes, and when Miss Emily, the last of the Duncombes, died, the village was inherited by a distant relative, who did not want it. This meant that the houses and other buildings in the village were divided into lots and auctioned off bit by bit.

The sale of the various houses and land, held at The Cross Keys Hotel, St Neots, made national news as it was not often that a whole village came onto the market. However, the houses and land were to be sold off by lot. The Galitzines decided that The Red House would make a nice country bolt-hole and some time during the 1940s, they gave up the Elm Tree Road house and moved to Waresley full time. Margaret Hodgson, Elena's mother, now in her 80s, also lived at The Red House in the early 1940s.

On Margaret Hodgson's death certificate for 1945, Pauline Dennistoun-Sword is named as the informant, which either meant she was living at The Red House, a former gardener's cottage, full time, or had gone there to look after her grandmother in her dying days. This seems to indicate that she had a close relationship with her grandmother. On the death certificate for Princess Elena Galitzine just three years later, Pauline is once again named as the informant.

8

The second husband

I T COULD BE that Pauline was made homeless by the fact that her brand-new husband was called up just a fortnight after their wedding at Aldershot and had no choice but go back to live with her parents. There are no traceable addresses for her between 1939 and 1945 and I imagine she was also living at The Red House, which would have been quite crowded with four adults there. Once again, there is no mention of her son who, for the time being, simply seems to have vanished.

Possibly because of his war record, we know far more about Pauline's second husband than her first. During the 1940s and 50s he was very well liked in Waresley: his interest in cricket, and in taking parts in the plays that Prince Nicholas put on at the village hall, made him extremely popular with the villagers, and some older residents still have memories of him.

Colin Dennistoun-Sword was educated at Harrow and was a keen sportsman. Elm Tree Road backs onto the Lord's cricket ground and it is likely that Pauline met him at cricket matches, as she was also keen on cricket although there is no evidence that she actually played. Colin had two sisters, Zoe and Eleanor, and by all accounts grew up in a close and happy home in Sussex. A year after he entered Lincoln's Inn as a trainee barrister, he joined the Gordon Highlanders as a Supplementary Reserve Officer and later, became a Lieutenant with the 1st Battalion. This 1st

Battalion was sent to France as part of the British Expeditionary Force and remained there until May 1940 when they were forced to surrender at St Valéry-en-Caux. Colin was seriously wounded in both legs and as such, not fit to be marched into captivity. He was taken firstly to Oflag VIB in Warburg, Westphalia, where he spent most of the time in hospital, and then transferred to Oflag VIIB Eichstadt in 1942.

An 'Oflag' (German: Offizierslager) was a type of German prisoner of war camp for officers only. A certain number of NCOs were allowed in Oflags to work as orderlies and look after the officers but generally speaking, an Oflag was considered a superior type of camp for the upper ranks of the armed forces.

According to Article 49 of the Geneva convention, all physically fit POWs below the rank of sergeant had to earn their keep and were put to work farming, mining or doing other heavy manual tasks, usually under harsh conditions, and held in separate camps known as Stalags. Senior NCOs could not be compelled to work although some of them chose to rather than having nothing to do.

Another POW at Oflag VIB in Warburg at the same time as Colin was Roger Mortimer, the journalist whose letters to his troublesome son, *Dear Lupin*, became an international best-seller and a West End play. Mortimer was always an indefatigable letter writer and in 2020 his son Charlie published his father's POW letters to a friend, Peggy Dunne. There is no record of Roger and Colin, both educated at top public schools—Roger at Eton—and commissioned into crack regiments, ever meeting each other at Oflag VIB, possibly because Colin was in hospital for most of this time.

But Roger's letters give a lively, quite upbeat account of what it was like to be a POW in a German camp. His missives were relentlessly cheerful in tone and he manages to put the best face on his captivity. He seemed to receive a lot of books to read and commented on them in his letters. In December 1941 he writes to Peggy: 'Provided I'm not in prison for long, I think it may have done me a certain amount of good. Anyway, I feel in much better form than last year.'

These young men had no idea how long they would be prisoners and did what they could to make the best of it. They staged plays and entertainments and in 1941 put on a performance of *Cinderella*. Roger writes: 'We had a very successful pantomime here; the 'heroine' was really disconcertingly feminine, almost frighteningly so, and Charlie Hopetoun was superb as an Ugly Sister.'

The 'Charlie Hopetoun' referred to was otherwise the third Marquess of Linlithgow. He was taken prisoner in 1940 with the 51st Highland Division and later held at Oflag IV-C, otherwise known as Colditz, one of the 'prominente', the name given to high profile prisoners who were held for possible use as hostages. Charlie was awarded the Military Cross and later became a prominent stockbroker.

Roger also wrote to Peggy in June 1942 about growing flowers in the prison: 'The flower garden outside our hut has been most successful.' The prisoners grew cornflowers, marigolds, zinnias and clarkia, Roger reveals. He does not say where they got the seeds, but such activities helped to make life bearable. Roger reveals to Peggy that he has a cold shower every day and a hot one once a week.

Colin, as an officer and a badly wounded one at that, would not have been able to work even if he had wanted to, and his injuries precluded him from joining in the football and other such games that the other officers played on makeshift pitches and grounds. So he decided to make good use of his time by completing his law exams. He was able to do this because the Red Cross organised distance learning whereby Prisoners of War were able to receive study material and exam papers from English universities and other seats of learning. At Oflag VIB Colin passed 'the elements of real property' examination, gaining a Class II, and his name appeared with that of other POWs in the Bar Examination Results in *The Times* in October 1942. Six months later he gained a Class One pass for Roman Law. By this time, he had been transferred to Oflag VIIB at Eichstadt.

Now this is where Pauline comes back in—or does she? One of the requirements for qualifying as a barrister, then as now, is that you have to eat a certain number of dinners at your particular Inn of Court. In his comprehensive account *St Valéry and its Aftermath: The*

Gordon Highlanders captured in France in 1940, author Stewart Mitchell says that, because clearly Colin could not eat these dinners while incarcerated in Germany, his wife Pauline ate them on his behalf. This information was obtained from Colin's obituary in *The Gordon Highlanders' Regimental Journal*. However, in her book, *The Barbed-Wire University*, detailing the lives and academic successes of prisoners of war, Midge Gillies says that Lincoln's Inn has no record of this.

It seems inherently unlikely and the most probable explanation is that Colin and the other POWs training to be barristers would be excused this arcane ritual under the peculiar circumstances in which they attempted to qualify.

The idea behind the distance learning was that these young men whose professional training had been interrupted by the war would be able to slot straight back into a solid occupation without having to start from scratch on returning home. Therefore, they would not have wasted their time while being held as POWs and would be able to earn a living on release. Very many took advantage of this opportunity, gaining degrees and other professional qualifications while in prison, and as one POW remarked: 'There were some damned clever chaps among the prisoners.'

Colin was one of these clever chaps and, by applying himself rigorously to his studies, was called to the Bar in absentia in the summer of 1944. It was only officers who were able to avail themselves of this distance learning and they were mightily grateful for the Red Cross for organising this, as well as the longed-for parcels that would arrive containing tins of food and other necessities and luxuries. Midge Gillies describes in her book how many lives were saved by the extra calories and vitamins that were received in the food parcels and that the cardboard packaging and string were equally useful in enabling the prisoners to devise entertainments, such as making stage sets for the plays that were performed.

Many of us have potent images of prisoners of war from a number of feature films such as *The Great Escape*, where Steve McQueen's hero, or anti-hero, plays a cunning and opportunistic escapee. This 1963 film, based on a true story, dramatised the mass escape of British Commonwealth POWs from Stalag Luft III, and for many film-goers, gave an abiding picture of daring, adventurous, stiff upper lip POWs that lasts until this day. It is true that many POWs did try to escape and some succeeded but for young men like Colin, any prospect of escape was impossible. He was too badly wounded even to try and it is unlikely that he received the very best medical attention while a prisoner, to the extent that his severe wounds never properly healed.

Life at Harrow may have prepared him to some extent for an uncomfortable, badly fed captive life and to make the best of whatever situation he found himself in, but those prisoner years took a serious toll that was never fully repaired. Apart from anything else, he did not even see a woman for five years and once again, although the all-male English boarding school life of the time would have meant he was used to a male-only world, he had only been married to an exciting, glamorous—and apparently rich—young woman for two weeks when he was called up. So, physically and emotionally, and possibly sexually, Colin suffered greatly during those captive years. In one of his letters home Roger Mortimer writes that the men wondered among themselves how many married women would remain faithful while their husbands were held as POWs and reckoned, around 45%.

We have no information as to whether Pauline was faithful for the five long years of her husband's captivity but given that she was a lively and attractive woman still under 30 and given that she was Pauline—very unlikely, I would say.

We know that she attended the funeral of her father-in-law, John Gow Dennistoun-Sword, in March 1945 as her name is given among the mourners. The funeral notice in the local paper says: 'His only son, Captain Colin Dennistoun-Sword, Gordon Highlanders, has been held as a Prisoner of War since June 1940.' Pauline must have wondered how long it would be before she could be reunited with him.

The Second World War ended on 9 September 1945 and Pauline and Colin found a home together at Artillery Mansions, Victoria. This imposing purpose-built Victorian mansion block contained a variety of apartments consisting of studio and one-, two- and three-bedroom flats. During the war the building had been commandeered as a Secret Intelligence Service Headquarters and after the war, was once again used as a private residence, in particular to house returning ex-servicemen. Colin and Pauline were named in electoral registers as living at apartment 3H in 1945 and 1946 when there is a gap and no London address is recorded for them for 1947 and 48. This would be, then, when they moved to The Red House Waresley to live there full time.

Pauline may have gone there initially to look after her mother, who was becoming seriously ill by now, and Colin went with her, partly because he was to all effects a brand-new husband and she had to get to know him all over again. What sort of young man would he be now, having endured such horrific experiences? He was still under 30 but in many ways, prematurely aged.

Princess Elena did not have long to live. In his little book *Waresley My Birthplace*, Oliver Broderick says that she was a cripple. I can find no evidence for this however and on her death certificate the cause of death was given as coronary thrombosis. Pauline Dennistoun-Sword was described as being in attendance at the death. Princess Elena was just 60 years old when she died, only three years after her mother, and her husband Prince Nicholas, now 50, was utterly heartbroken. Catherine Horwood-Barwise believed that theirs was a true and lasting love match, for all the differences in age, upbringing, background and class.

Her death notice, in *The Times*, reads as follows:

GALITZINE. On Oct. 20, 1948, after a long illness bravely borne, at The Red House, Waresley, near Sandy, Bedfordshire, Princess Elena Galitzine, beloved wife of Prince Nicholas Galitzine and mother of Yurka Galitzine and Pauline Dennistoun-Sword. Funeral at Waresley, Saturday, Oct. 23, at 3 pm. All flowers to Evans and Sons, Cambridge Street, St Neots, Hunts.

Elena's death meant many changes. In her Will, drawn up in 1943, she left The Red House to Pauline. When she died she left around £7000, about £300,000 in today's money, so not such a huge sum, but the Will, with many crossings-out and codicils, does not make clear whether this included the house, or whether it was cash at the bank. Her 'beloved husband' Prince Nicholas is not even mentioned, although there is a bequest to Yurka, and to her housekeeper, a local villager. The executor of her Will is named as Martins Bank in Liverpool.

At any rate, it meant some serious adjustments for Pauline, Colin and Prince Nicholas. Rather than making Nicholas homeless, Pauline and Colin offered to keep him on at the Red House and for this he was mightily grateful as he was already deeply embedded in Waresley life. There is no information available as to whether he was still working, but according to Philip Norman, he had a nice sideline in painting pub signs. He painted the sign for the Spread Eagle in Croxton, another village near to Waresley, and was part of an eccentric circle that used to meet in the pub. Among them, Philip said, was the 'mannish' Miss Minney, George Harrison, the son of Dr Ernest Harrison who had delivered the St Neots Quads, and his German-born wife Ilse.

George Harrison was not cut from the same cloth as his father. He originally tried fruit farming in Waresley, then went bankrupt and had to take a lowly manual job at the Vauxhall car factory in Luton. Thanks to his shenanigans and apparent inability to remain solvent, Ilse divorced him and herself then ran the Spread Eagle pub. She then married Dr Tony Ellis and went to live with her daughter Diana at Dr Ellis's house, Merton Grange, Gamlingay. This house is minutely described in Philip Norman's early novel, See Him Sweat, and in the event, Diana Harrison, later Scott, lived there until 2009 when the house was sold.

The question arises: how did Prince Nicholas get work painting pub signs? Although he had some artistic ability, this was not the main reason. During the war, many pub and village signs had been removed so as to confuse the Germans if they invaded. The result was that after the war, pubs had to have their signs repainted. In his book A Lesson in Art and Life: The Colourful World of Cedric Morris and Arthur Lett-Haines,

Hugh St Clair writes that in 1948 the Cobbold brewing family asked if any students from Morris and Lett-Haines' School of Painting and Drawing could paint new signs for their East Anglian pubs. There was such work for artists all over the country in the immediate postwar years and it is likely that Prince Nicholas was commissioned by local breweries to paint new pub signs. After all, having a real live Prince painting your signs gave the pubs quite some kudos. Unfortunately, most of those pubs, including the Spread Eagle, have long since vanished along with the signs.

As Colin had passed his law exams and was eligible to practise as a barrister, he of course had to work in London as there were no chambers in Waresley. Philip Norman remembered that Prince Nicholas drove a Morris Minor although others said that he drove an old-fashioned square-type Citroen. Maybe he drove both as I certainly recall Pauline motoring into town in a Morris Minor.

Whatever did she do with herself, one wonders, with Colin in London during the working week and Prince Nicholas painting pub signs? She certainly didn't have a job but one also wonders whether she began to regret her hasty marriage and being stuck with a permanently wounded husband. She clearly had to give him a chance and could not in all conscience divorce him so readily as she had her first husband.

As for Colin, he tried valiantly to establish himself as a barrister but this was not easy as he had returned to a country very different from the one he had left in 1939. Laws had changed, there were new customs and also, new crimes to be tried. The profession of barrister, although in many ways still stuck in the 18th century, was finally modernising and adapting itself to the new postwar situation. It was still pretty much men only, although the fast-rising barrister Rose Heilbron, later a QC, was finally showing that women could succeed at the Bar as well.

I've often wondered whether Pauline considered training as a barrister herself, but that might have been too much like hard work although the matter of her (possibly) eating dinners at Lincoln's Inn may have meant that she ate them on her own behalf, rather than that of her absentee husband. However, I doubt it, and am inclined to think it was one of those urban tales that became endlessly repeated until it acquired the patina of truth.

The law was still, immediately postwar, an elite male profession and the usual set-up would be that the solicitors, barristers and judges were all old Etonians or Harrovians or similar, and the criminals would come from the poor working classes. Although the trial of Victor Hervey and his gang proved that upper-class men could be criminals, it was still generally held that only the lower orders committed crimes.

This was, then, the barristers' world that Colin Dennistoun-Sword entered in late 1945. He came from the class that usually sat in judgment as it was only rich men, or men from rich families, that could afford to train as barristers. But when you have been out of your country for five years, with only minimal information getting through to your prison camp, it is not a simple matter to slot into a highly competitive and rigorous profession that needs a thorough, and current, knowledge of the law. The exams that Colin had passed at the camps were theoretical; he now had to try to put them to practical use. How, for instance, was Roman Law relevant when dealing with motoring offences or black-market racketeers?

Colin also returned to civilian life emaciated, in poor health and bewildered, to a London he did not recognise. Many once famous landmarks had been devastated by bombing, and there were shops and houses with no windows, gaps where buildings had once been and rubble and dust everywhere. And there was no counselling or therapy available. Apart from trying to get going in his profession, Colin had not been able to attend his father's funeral and in addition, many of his fellow Gordon Highlanders had been killed. All in all, it was not going to be easy for Colin and Pauline to pull together, although there is every indication that they tried, and village life seemed to suit Colin as well.

Waresley had been completely untouched by the war and seemed to retain every trace of a pre-war Merrie England, with its one pub,

The Duncombe Arms, its church, village school and its cricket on the green. It all provided a kind of rehabilitation for Colin, where he could gradually come back to life and forget the horrors and privations he had witnessed, or at least, allow them to fade away.

He soon became popular and the Waresleyites took him to their hearts. He organised sideshows for the village fêtes, took part in plays produced by his stepfather-in-law Prince Nicholas Galitzine and—most of all—became a prominent member of the cricket club. He was pleased to see that Waresley Cricket Club punched above its weight and belonged to a higher league than was usual for a tiny village club.

Colin was directly involved in Waresley Cricket Club between 1949 and 1953 as a player and after that as Vice-President, secretary and treasurer. He was for a time Vice-Captain of the team although his former cricket prowess was severely hampered by his injuries. I have a scrap of a letter written by him in the early 1950s where he writes: 'I am glad to see efforts being made to encourage the boys of the village to play cricket.'

One of those boys was John Gillett, who grew up in the neighbouring village of Great Gransden, but who was drawn to Waresley because of its cricket. Much of its success in the 1950s was down to Colin, and John, now in his eighties, remembers those days: 'Cricket was my great love as a boy, and Colin Dennistoun-Sword did all he could to coach the village lads. He used to take us to St Neots for extra coaching. Although Colin couldn't get about all that well because of his war injuries, you could still see the quality in his cricket.

'I understand that he had played for his old school in the Eton versus Harrow matches. He was very decent, very kind to us boys and sometimes we wondered why he took such an interest as he was clearly from a much higher social class than we were.'

And what about Pauline? 'She was a very different matter,' John said. 'In 1954 I was called up for National Service and when I came back, I found that Pauline had left him and married somebody else. I wasn't happy about that at all and it marked the end of Colin's active involvement with the cricket club.'

Pauline herself played an active part in the club and acted as scorer. Older Waresleyites remember her as always being heavily made up, chain-smoking and with a bottle of gin by her side. One can only hope that with all those accessories the scores were accurate. Colin Croot, who grew up in Waresley, and continued to live there all his life, reckoned he owed his position in the Second Eleven at Peterhouse, Cambridge, to Colin's early coaching. And Grahame Jackson, who lived next door to Pauline, also remembers this coaching and being taken to St Neots, where there was a much bigger cricket club.

Grahame also has a memory of Pauline shooting his father's drake when it had waddled across to her house. He said: 'I've never forgiven her for this and can't imagine why she did it. I know that she used to meet and exchange gossip with my stepmother, who was also called Pauline, and they often chatted to each other. But I never spoke to her after the shooting incident as it wasn't even sporting, shooting it on the ground.'

One reason, possibly, for Colin Dennistoun-Sword taking such an interest in the village lads' cricket prowess was because he could not have any children of his own. His war wounds had left him either impotent or infertile, and that was another abiding problem of trying to establish his life with Pauline. Although not unkind, she had nursed her mother and grandmother through their final illnesses and she was now having to cope with a severely disabled husband who was never going to get better; not what she thought she had signed up for when she fell in love with and married this formerly virile, sporty young man.

Moreover, Colin was having serious problems in continuing his career at the Bar as, increasingly, he was finding it difficult to stand up in court. So the shining future career which he had fondly envisaged when taking his exams in the prison camp—were they invigilated one wonders—was looking like a distant prospect.

But he was continuing to enjoy village life and in addition to the cricket, he became a member of the Waresley Gleaners, the Amateur Dramatic Society founded by the always theatrical and flamboyant

The Waresley Gleaners put on a production of See How they Run. Colin Dennistoun-Sword is the vicar on the far right. These plays were produced by Prince Nicholas Galitzine

Prince Nicholas. The plays were performed in the Waresley Village Hall and in surrounding villages during the 1950s. In one, *See How they Run*, a 1942 farce by Philip King, Colin played the part of the Reverend Lionel Troop. It suited him as it was a part he could play largely sitting down.

Both Colin and Prince Nicholas took part in village life to the full and were, as one might say, big fish in small ponds. Nicholas was looked up to as a member of Russian royalty and very much enjoyed playing the part of Lord of the Manor. He was also something of a prankster, painting his house red, which is how it acquired its name, and removing the wrought iron structure from the top of the memorial lamp in front of the village pub and replacing it with a tractor tyre.

The point of this prank has not been recorded, but there was an outcry in the village and the Prince had the ironwork welded back on. He is also remembered for twirling his handlebar moustache for dramatic effect. Colin was regarded with much affection as well although perhaps the same could not be said for Pauline. She had a reputation for being 'flighty' and most of the villagers remained somewhat wary.

She was not, surprisingly, the only glamorous woman in Waresley. The other one was Winifred 'Bunty' Redman, the slim, attractive wife of Colonel Jack Redman of Waresley Park. But the difference between the two was that Bunty was a local woman, whose family was well known in the area. Bunty was also a regular customer in my mother's shop and when I remarked how slim she was, Mum replied: 'Yes but she starves herself to do it', thus proving that, even in the 1950s, dieting was nothing new. Pauline was also concerned to retain her elegant figure unlike her mother Princess Elena, who put on quite a lot of weight towards the end of her life. The two women, Bunty and Pauline, knew each other as both their husbands were into cricket and both the wives were into flower arranging. But whereas Bunty was fondly regarded by the villagers, nobody knew what to make of Pauline.

There were rumours going around that Bunty was having affairs but while they remained rumours, those concerning Pauline were true. For some time she had been having an affair with Colonel Oliver Sismey, of Offord Cluny Manor.

She had started to feel that she had given the marriage to Colin a fair go and although she had originally only come to Waresley to look after her mother and then her grandmother, the fact was she had been stuck in the village for ten years. She had to escape.

One day she whispered to my mother: 'Don't tell anybody, but I'm going to marry Oliver Sismey.'

Picking herself up off the floor, metaphorically, Mum said: 'Colonel Sismey? But aren't you still married to Mr Dennistoun-Sword?'

'Oh,' said Pauline, 'we are getting divorced.'

This was 1955, when divorces in St Neots and district were extremely rare. And naturally, Mum could not keep the secret to herself. She told her crony Dora Mildren, another gentleman farmer's wife and from the rich Banks farming family in Waresley. 'That doesn't surprise me,' Dora said. 'She's been carrying on with Oliver Sismey for ages, going over to his house and coming back late at night. I don't know how Colin puts up with it but you know how easy going he is. I expect he will agree to divorce Pauline; she always gets her own way.'

Dora was right. In 1956, Pauline and Oliver Sismey ran away to London to get married, and that meant another name change. First she was Pauline Turner, then Pauline Galitzine, then Pauline Daubeny, then Pauline Dennistoun-Sword and finally, Pauline Sismey. She brazened it out to go and live with her new husband at Offord Cluny Manor. As a result, The Red House was sold—it belonged to Pauline after all—and Colin and Prince Nicholas Galitzine became homeless. Colin went back to live at Artillery Mansions and Prince Nicholas lived in a London flat belonging to his son Prince Yurka.

By this time, Colin had realised that the life of a barrister was not for him as he could no longer stand up in court and he became a professional genealogist instead, co-founding the firm Deeny and Sword.

'I was not happy at all when Colin left,' said John Gillett, 'but luckily he agreed to keep up his connection with the Cricket Club, which lasted until 1976. It was a sad day for us and for Waresley cricket, when Colin left to go and live in London.'

Waresley also was going to miss Prince Nicholas Galitzine, who had added so much colour and vivacity to village life.

9

The third husband

ON 27 April 1956, Oliver North Deane Sismey aged 55 married Pauline Vincent Dennistoun-Sword, aged 44, at Kensington Register Office. The 'condition' of both parties was named as 'previous marriage dissolved'. The groom's rank or profession was listed as Lieutenant-Colonel, HM Army, retired.

The couple gave different addresses. Oliver's was 59 Egerton Gardens, sw3 and Pauline's was 2a Sydney Close, sw3; both South Kensington addresses. Oliver's father was named as George Herbert Sismey, a solicitor, and Pauline's father, once again, was down as Henry Stanley Turner, deceased, and of private means.

The two witnesses at the wedding were J.H.B. Heathcote and Yurka Galitzine.

The fact that Pauline gave a London address—in a very expensive street—indicates that by this time The Red House had been sold, and poor old Colin and Prince Nicholas evicted. I'm sure this must be so as, once the newly-weds came back from honeymoon, they went to live at Oliver's ancestral home, Offord Cluny Manor, an imposing 17th century residence on the road from St Neots to Huntingdon. It had been in the Sismey family for over 300 years and it was rumoured that Oliver Cromwell had stayed there during the Civil War.

So when Pauline bolted, she did not bolt very far; only around ten miles or a 15-minute car journey.

Oliver and Pauline Sismey at a dinner, 1961

She must, though, have thought she was considerably bettering herself by marrying Oliver Sismey, who had not remarried since his own divorce in the 1930s. For much of that time he had lived in the Manor with his elderly father, who, on learning of his son's impending second marriage, moved into a care home. It is not recorded what he thought of this adventuress, this Evelyn Waugh character, already twice divorced, this local equivalent of Mrs Simpson, shedding men all over the place, who was going to be taking over as the chatelaine of the house, which had not seen a woman's touch since Oliver's first wife had moved out more than 20 years earlier.

In fact, Oliver, who had been educated at Eton, and Colin, educated at Harrow, were from similar backgrounds and had similar military careers. Also, both of their fathers were solicitors.

They were very different characters, though. Whereas Colin was, in spite of his war wounds, go-ahead and modern, particularly after starting his genealogy company, Oliver was what we would now call old school; tweedy, fusty and at 55, much older than his years. To me he seemed a very old man, shuffling around while Pauline did all the talking (and drinking!) and entertaining. Had she told him, one wonders, about her early years (still a mystery) and the son who nobody had seen or heard anything of?

Oliver's background was extremely traditional and after Eton, he went to the royal Military Academy, Sandhurst. He joined the King's Royal Rifle Corps where he progressed from Captain in 1930 to Major in 1939. He had a distinguished war record and in August 1942, now with the rank of Lieutenant-Colonel, was in command of the 2nd

Battalion in North Africa until he was replaced by Lieutenant-Colonel William Heathcoat-Amory on 24 August 1942. By then Montgomery was in overall command of the 8th Army, which defeated Rommel in the Second Battle of El-Alamein in November 1942.

There are no records of Colonel Sismey being wounded or captured, so we must assume he returned to Offord Cluny Manor in good health and good spirits. In October 1931 he had married Anna Laetitia Philips, the daughter of a Brigadier, when he was 31 and she was 18. To today's young generation, the prospect of being married at 18 is little short of horrific but it was quite common at the time, especially among the upper classes, in Barbara Cartland novels come to life.

A typical scenario would be that a young man would establish himself and sow his wild oats and then, in his early 30s, look around for a suitable victim to marry; with any luck, a young naïve virgin who did not know any better. The last such aristocratic union was between Lady Diana Spencer and Prince (now King) Charles, and we all know what happened to that marriage.

The problem for these much older men was that these very young girls didn't stay young and naïve. They grew up, looked around and asked themselves: what on earth have I done? They had married a man they hardly knew, just because he had, or appeared to have, money and prospects, and within a year of marriage they frequently found themselves mothers as well, while still teenagers. This is exactly what happened to Oliver Sismey's 12 years younger wife. Before long she fled, taking their infant daughter with her, and Oliver was left, after only two or three years of marriage, a single man again.

In 1950, Oliver's daughter and only child Islay had been presented at court, much as Pauline had herself been 20 years earlier, and two years later, following her mother's example, married a man 15 years her senior. This was Major Francis Michael Edwards, later Lieutenant-Colonel and once again, an Army man and a career officer. Francis, considered an urbane and witty man, had been taken prisoner during a defence of the sector of the Dunkirk perimeter in May 1940, and after repeated attempts to escape from other camps, was sent to Oflag

IVC, otherwise known as Colditz Castle. Francis was just one year older than Colin Dennistoun-Sword and they may even have been held in the same Oflags. None of Francis's attempts to escape were successful and like Colin, he was held as a POW for five years.

After his divorce, Oliver remained a bachelor until Pauline set her sights on him. She too, it will be remembered, had first married at 19 but she was now a mature woman in her forties and ready to take on a new husband, a huge house and extensive gardens rather than flitting about in her Morris Minor doing not very much. By the time Oliver remarried he had retired from the Army and was living the life of a country gentleman, pottering about. By this time he had no particular occupation but Pauline was definitely going to give him one. Oliver did not need to work because not long after the marriage his father died and left him the house and around £2 million in today's equivalent. Also, he had his Army pension. By selling The Red House, Pauline also brought in some money to the household.

She soon got into her stride, having successfully dispatched husband no. 2. The village she moved to was only about seven miles away from Waresley but was slightly larger. There were actually two Offords: Offord Cluny and Offord D'Arcy, named in the 13th century as they had connections with France. Altogether there were about 1000 inhabitants in the two Offords, so in a sense Pauline was moving to 'the bright lights,' added to which she could now legitimately become the Lady of the Manor, a title she had not been able to secure for herself in Waresley, much as Prince Nicholas Galitzine was regarded as Lord of the Manor during his years there.

The house that Pauline now moved into was extremely grand but in a sad state of neglect, and she had to do what she could about making it into a home. She was, it has to be said, a kind of intruder and if Waresley villagers never really took her to their hearts, it was going to be even more of an uphill struggle to win over residents of the Offords. She was muscling in on a man's house and had to try to feminise it and make it more comfortable. Unlike the Red House, which was hers, she was now an interloper.

When the former Henrietta Tiarks was married to the Duke of Bedford, she often complained that she was living in a man's house, one that had been designed for male aristocrats, and she never really felt at home there. Offord Cluny Manor was not quite so grand as Woburn Abbey but it would be, to many women, similarly forbidding with its wide sweeping staircase, portraits of ancestors, four-poster beds and antique furniture. Moving into a man's ancestral home is by no means the same as a couple buying a house together and it was necessary to tread carefully to establish some kind of ownership of the place. Also, it was a house that really needed servants and although there were five attics originally designed as servants' quarters, these had not been used for years. All help was hired from the village.

The house was much too large, really, for two middle-aged people and the sensible thing would have been to sell it and move to somewhere smaller but it was Oliver's family home and he refused to budge.

'I've told the Colonel that it would be sensible to sell the place and move to somewhere smaller, but he won't hear of it,' Pauline said to my mother. She always called him 'the Colonel' in front of people she considered his social inferiors.

So far, my mother had only driven past it but it was to become almost her second home once Pauline got going. 'I expect it needs a lot doing to it,' Mum said. 'After all, the Colonel has been living there by himself all these years.'

'Yes but I know I will never persuade him to move so I'm going to turn it into a paying proposition.'

'How are you going to do that?"

'Apart from the market garden—and I'm going to study gardening books—I'm thinking of opening the gardens to the public.'

Here my mother was sceptical as she maintained there was nothing to see and who on earth would pay to look round the Offord Cluny Manor gardens. Every year she went to the Chelsea Flower Show, so knew what show gardens could look like. Pauline also went to the Chelsea Flower Show each year but unlike my mother, who just paid a day visit, Pauline stayed in her London club.

My mother said nothing about Pauline's aspirations, mainly because although she made fun of Pauline behind her back, when confronted with her face to face, she was always slightly in awe of her. Pauline was bold, whereas basically my mother was timid; partly because it was her nature and partly because people from the working class were expected to know their place and not speak out of turn.

Pauline was always very sociable and although not a great cook, soon began holding dinner parties for the local gentry, hiring one of the village women to come and prepare meals. And, of course, the drink flowed. By all accounts, the Colonel had a fine cellar.

And what she had told my mother about running a market gardening company and opening the gardens to the public was no empty boast. Before long, this formerly bone-idle mistress of the Red House was studying gardening books, employing the locals as gardeners and delivery men and becoming conversant with the kind of vegetables that would grow well on the estate. It was as if, finally, she had found a role for herself and one that suited her. Shortly after her marriage, she became President of the Buckden Gardeners' Association. Buckden is a large village about three miles from Offord Cluny.

Although the 1939 newspaper report of her second marriage stated that she was 'a clever linguist', she never seemed to do anything with her languages. Perhaps of course, it was a matter of confidence. My own take on this was that her confidence had taken a severe battering during the war, when her husband of only two weeks was snatched away from her, and she then had to assume the role of carer for her grandmother and mother, and after that keep house for a couple of men. Maybe it was not the life she would have chosen or expected, but once she married the Colonel, she came into her own.

It was as if Offord Cluny Manor suited her. At any rate, much to my mother's surprise, Pauline became a tough and efficient business-woman. 'I would never have thought she had it in her,' Mum would say to her confidant Dora Mildren. 'She came in with two huge sacks of runner beans the other day. I don't know how she expects me to sell them.'

Pauline Sismey (in the dark hat) presents a basket of flowers to Lady Sandwich at the Buckden Gardeners' Association annual show, 1961

'I'm as surprised as you,' Dora said. Dora was another of these women who did nothing at all. She was married to local farmer Ellis Mildren and they lived at Manor Farm, Hail Weston, yet another tiny village about two miles from St Neots. Dora and Ellis were childless and doted on dogs instead. She added: 'I just wonder how long THAT marriage will last.'

The general consensus was that the Colonel was a sitting duck, ripe for some gold-digging woman to come and claim him. He was as surprised as anybody else when this lady of leisure he had married became a businesswoman. One wonders whether here there might have been some throwback to the grandfather she had never met, the fruit merchant John Fawcett-Hodgson from Liverpool. Perhaps also her grandmother Margaret Fawcett-Hodgson had imparted some information about how to run a successful business. She had, after all, run a boarding house after she was widowed.

'She must have a lot of help with the garden,' said my mother to Dora, 'because she always looks immaculate.'

'You know she has her hair done every single day,' Dora said.

'She would have to because there is never a hair out of place. I wish I could bring myself to tell her not to park her car in the middle of the road, though. People hoot at her all the time but she never takes any notice.'

'You know what my word is for her,' said Dora. 'Eccentric. The rules that apply to other people don't apply to her.'

Oliver's father had died in his nursing home in 1958; a year that marked another great change for my mother. While Pauline was busy getting her market gardening business going and yes, she did open the gardens to the public under some scheme, the owner of Paxton Park Nurseries, Mrs Bradshaw, was going to sell up.

Paxton Park was earmarked to be turned into a housing estate and so both the shop and the nursery would be up for sale and not as a going concern. Mum could not afford to buy the shop from Mrs Bradshaw and, after more than ten years of working as a manager, wondered what she was going to do. She obviously had to do something to earn a living; there was no possibility of sitting at home baking cakes and dusting furniture.

She heard that a couple of new shops were going to be built by the council in Cambridge Street and decided to apply for the lease on one of them. The type of business that would be carried on was at the discretion of the council. There was also going to be a two-bedroom flat above the shops. A Mr and Mrs Pindred, from Brampton, a village about two miles from Huntingdon, had applied to run a grocery business at one of the shops and Mum applied to run a florist's business at the other.

The only problem was: if she was successful in her application, where was the money going to come from to buy the lease, equip the shop and buy a van for deliveries? For although Mum had, presumably, been earning a reasonable wage, she had no savings at all. It would also be difficult, if not impossible, for a woman to get a bank loan to start a business. If Dad had been of the slightest use, he might have been able to obtain one for her but as it was, the only answer here was to treat him as the child he essentially was and leave him completely out of the process.

She mentioned her predicament to Dora Mildren, who said: 'Don't worry. Ellis and I can lend you the money for the lease and to stock the shop.'

'Really? You mean it?'

'Yes, I wouldn't like to see the only decent florist in the town disappear and you can pay us back when you can. It's a no-interest loan, by the way.' Mum was so grateful to the Mildrens, so much so that when Ellis died a year later, she frequently put flowers on his grave in remembrance of that kind act which came exactly when needed.

There was more to come. One of the local solicitors, Guy Walmisley-Dresser, offered to do the conveyancing at mates' rates as he had been so grateful for the help and advice given to his wife Sybil when she was just getting going with her flower arrangement hobby. And so, after a few heart-stopping moments when the council was not sure it wanted to lease a brand-new shop to a mere woman, and up against some competition from other businesspeople who wanted to open a shop in Cambridge Street, she won the day and opened her new shop under the name M.C. Garrett.

Paxton Park Nurseries had gone for ever and Mum also devised a new slogan: 'Flowers for all occasions.' She wanted to drop the palette logo and slogan 'The Artists in Flowers', saying 'I think mine is just as good.'

From the start, the new shop was a success. Mum obviously needed staff and employed the 15-year-old Thelma George, from Godmanchester. She had some slight misgivings as Thelma's father was a florist, and worried that she might reveal some of the secrets of the trade that would be passed on, especially as her customer base extended to Godmanchester, but her fears proved unfounded and Thelma, who became a friend for life, turned out to be gold dust. Mum also needed a driver and employed Laetitia Overton, who also often used to go over to Pauline Sismey's and sit in the kitchen gossiping over cups of coffee and gin—well, the gin was for Pauline.

Pauline also showed her solicitous side. Mum was highly aller-gic to wasp stings and that was a particular bugbear in the summer, especially around flowers. Once, Pauline came into the shop to find my mother with a face severely swollen and feeling dizzy from a very severe reaction.

'I think I will have to go to the doctor,' Mum said.

'No, don't do that. I'm going to bring you in some special stuff which will work wonders and you are ordered to use it. If I find you haven't been using it I will come and dump 200 pounds of beans on you.'

Mum was amused at this in spite of her struggles with the wasp sting. Pauline duly brought in her magic remedy and whether or not it worked I don't know but she never carried out her threat of bringing in a lorry load of beans. She also now took an interest in me.

'What's Elizabeth going to do as a career?' she asked, careers for girls by now having become more standard. 'Will she be going on to university?'

'Yes, I expect so,' Mum said.

'She's not going to be working in the shop, then?'

'Oh I doubt it.'

When Mum mentioned to Dora Mildren that I was thinking of going to university, she was not impressed at all. She said: 'I only wanted to help my mother. Elizabeth doesn't seem to want to do that.'

'She never helps in the house,' Mum said. That, sadly, was true. Because she worked full time, Mum had always employed a cleaner called, appropriately, Mrs Tidy. This meant I was not expected to help with housework, but Mum often warned me darkly, 'You won't avoid the kitchen sink all your life.' Sadly, she was right, there.

Dora, for all her championing of Mum—and the loan was paid back very quickly—wanted me to remain in my lowly station. The idea of going to university was an alien concept for these farmers' wives. University was in their view for boys only, as girls 'were only going to get married and have children, so their education would be wasted.' That was the popular view at the time, added to which, the prospect of a mere shopkeeper's daughter going to university shook up the rich and leisured gentlemen farmer fraternity. It meant that the lower orders really were getting above themselves, perish the thought.

There was a long way to go before feminism infiltrated St Neots. But Mum's customers were becoming more interested in me as my teenage years sped by. Joan Furbank, for instance, a former hairdresser, would take me to John Cornel's hair salon in Cambridge, where Susan Bath, a farmer's daughter from Cross Hall, St Neots, worked. Joan also started to see me as a fount of knowledge.

She came into the shop one day when I was there and mentioned that she was entering a flower arrangement competition and had decided on a *Macbeth* theme; not easy, I would have thought, to render into flowers unless she was going to depict Birnam Wood going to Dunsinane. 'I've been making the witches,' she said to me. 'Do you think I can get away with two of them?'

I was studying *Macbeth* for A-level, so I said: 'No, I don't think so. The very first line of the play is: "When shall we three meet again?"'

'Damn' she said. 'If I was my father, I would say, bugger. Do you really think I will have to make three witches? Won't two give the idea?'

'I would make the three of them,' I advised. She did and later came into the shop to say that she had won the competition and the three witches were much admired. I'm not sure whether she made them out of flowers or eye of newt and toe of frog, but she was grateful for the advice, and thereafter regarded me as some kind of literary genius. Joan Furbank was also very kind to Philip Norman and encouraged his writing and gift for drawing. When she died, Philip wrote an affectionate tribute in the *Daily Mail*.

I went into the sixth form at Huntingdon Grammar School and started to apply for university. I needed referees and Guy Walmisley-Dresser and Colonel Sismey obliged. One evening I went over to Offord Cluny Manor with Mum, bearing the papers that Oliver Sismey had to sign as a referee. I was going to study law, and as Oliver was filling in the form, Pauline asked me: 'What is a tortfeasor?'

'A criminal?' I said. 'A wrongdoer?' I thought my Latin might help me here, as 'tortus' in Latin means twisted, or wrong.

'Very good,' said Pauline, although how on earth she expected me to know any legal terms when as yet I had not studied any law, I have no idea. Perhaps she just wanted to show off her knowledge of legal terms while her husband was acting as my sponsor. 'A tort is a civil wrong' she explained. I had no idea at the time how she might know that.

She asked me which universities I was applying to and I said, Durham and Nottingham.

'Not Cambridge?' Cambridge seemed obvious I suppose as it was only 16 miles away. Durham and Nottingham, so far as most St Neots people were concerned, were in the frozen North; uncharted territory to any of them. The nearest they got to the North of England was listening to Yorkshire broadcaster Wilfred Pickles presenting *Have a Go* on the radio.

'Not at the moment,' I replied, adding, 'You have to do another year in the sixth form and take the Cambridge exam.'

'Why not aim high?'

I was slightly nervous of Pauline, as many people were. 'I might,' I said. 'See how A-levels go.'

She continued to probe. 'Are you going to be a barrister, or a solicitor?'

'A solicitor I expect,' I said. At this point I had no real idea what a barrister was, although I had met a few solicitors.

'My ex-husband was a barrister. I can tell you, it's a very tough profession.'

'Yes, I can imagine.' All I knew about barristers at this time was that they appeared in court wearing wigs and robes.

'Have a fag,' Pauline offered, holding out a cigarette packet. I accepted. I was a grown-up now and had already started smoking. 'Thanks,' I said, taking one.

'Have you got a boyfriend?' she asked.

'Yes' I said. I was going out, if you could call it that, with Alex Williams, a student at St Martin's School of Art.

'That's good,' she said. 'Just get your career going before you have any thoughts of marriage.'

Nothing was further from my mind than being married to art student Alex, but I assured her that I had no ambitions in that direction just yet. All the while, Oliver Sismey said nothing except for, 'I think that's all for these forms,' and handed them back to me. 'Thank you very much,' I said, pleased that I had got such pillars of the community to be my referees; surely that would help with my application.

I had not known at the time, of course, that Pauline had both solicitors and barristers in her background. But actually, although I did not enlighten her, I had no real intention of becoming either a solicitor or a barrister. I just thought that after two years of intensive study of English literature for A-level, it would be good to have a change and equip myself with some knowledge of the law. I still hankered after being a famous writer; an ambition I was careful to keep to myself for fear of the hoots of laughter that would ensue, as there were no known writers in the whole of Huntingdonshire. Actually, that was not quite true as the novelist and non-fiction writer David Garnett lived at Hilton Hall, near St Ives, but he was almost the exception that proved the rule as there was also a local Buckden writer, Frances Turk, who sat in a shed at the bottom of her garden and churned out many romances for the publishers Robert Hale. Frances was single, lived with her parents and herself had no known romantic liaisons. So it was all imagination, and one of my Buckden friends said disparagingly, 'Her novels are the sort where lovers disappear into the potting shed dot dot dot.'

If the locals knew of my ambitions, or that I actually hobnobbed with David Garnett and his daughters, they would still shake their heads and mutter: 'I hear that Mrs Garrett's daughter wants to be a famous writer!' Talk about getting above your station!

In the event, I was offered a place at Durham University to study law and I took it. My ambition to go to Girton had somewhat faded, as I was by now desperate to leave home, and the fact that there were, at the time, around 3000 places a year at Cambridge for men and only

300 for women, made it an outside chance indeed that I would get in. The headmaster, Mr Rowntree, wanted me to stay on and take the Oxbridge exam as I had brilliant A-level results along with my two best friends Kate Hadley (who was later to join me in Fleet Street) and Vicky Darnell, but my feeling was that I still had little hope of getting in and I did not want to spend another year hanging about St Neots.

Already, townsfolk were gossiping among themselves. 'Isn't Mrs Garrett's daughter ever going to leave school? About time she went out and earned some money.'

When our A-level results were announced, the teachers said: 'The rebels have done well' as we had fancied ourselves left bank intellectuals, hanging out with Simone de Beauvoir and Jean-Paul Sartre in Paris pavement cafes. Pretentious, *nous?*

I already felt I had come a long way from my lowly origins, quite literally as well, since Durham University was 300 miles away from St Neots. Once at university, though, I soon found that law did not suit me, and I quickly changed to reading English, although I was grateful for having some smattering of legal knowledge. It did not come amiss.

My mother's social circle widened. She joined the Kimbolton and District Flower Arrangement Society, founded by local doctor's wife Phyllis Kilby. All the local flower grandees joined, including Dora Mildren, Sybil Walmisley-Dresser, Mrs Ramply of Southoe, Joan Furbank—who was to become famous in the flower arranging world, meriting an obituary in the *Telegraph*—and of course, Pauline Sismey. The Flower Arrangement Society meant more business for Mum and a wider reach for those practising this fast-burgeoning art.

The founding of the Flower Club (still going and still meeting in the Mandeville Hall in 2023) meant that before long, more ordinary women were becoming interested in flower arranging and one might have thought that Mum would be pleased at the gradual democratization of this once upper-class pursuit, but no. She complained that 'common people' were now infiltrating flower arranging, and that it was losing its exclusivity. Why, even women from council houses were entering flower arrangement competitions. It would never do!

By now, the roles between Pauline and my mother were pretty much reversed. Pauline often came into the shop with deliveries from her market garden, still parking in the middle of the road although by now the Morris Minor had been exchanged for a smart van—and she became ever more gossipy and confiding.

It must have been about 1962 or 3 when she came into the shop and said that her son was engaged to be married. This was the first time she had ever mentioned a son, and we certainly knew he wasn't the fruit of her union with Colin Dennistoun-Sword.

She did not enlighten us as to who his father was, but went on about the fiancée: 'She's a lovely girl, very natural. She was wearing a dress that you wouldn't know whether it was cheap or expensive. But I'm so happy for him.'

'Where did this son come from?' Mum asked Dora Mildren. 'Did you know anything about a son?'

'Well, yes, in a way. Maggie Minney used to be quite friendly with her, and she told me that Mrs Sismey had a son from a long way back. Must have been, you know,' Dora whispered, 'out of wedlock. I reckon she's got a past, that woman. None of us know much about her.'

After the engagement, this 'lovely girl' often used to stay at Offord Cluny Manor, according to Pauline, presumably with the son, although I never saw either and they certainly never came into the shop.

A class point, or perhaps a 1950s custom, was that however friendly Mum was with her customers, they were always 'Mrs'; first names were never used. The only exception was for Margaret Minney, whom everybody called Maggie, perhaps because she did not fit neatly into masculine or feminine, and to call a middle-aged woman who looked exactly like a man 'Miss' sounded odd. Generally speaking, adults only used first names with relatives, people they had known in childhood, or with those who were much younger.

Since this son has finally made, not exactly an appearance, but has been acknowledged at least, it is perhaps time to delve into his history and discover why Pauline never once mentioned him until he was adult, and old enough to be engaged to be married.

A garden fête held on Friday 13 August 1935 at Cosgrove Hall. Front: Penelope Winterbottom, Arthur Noble, Princess Elena Galitzine, local vicar. Back: George Winterbottom, Pauline Daubeny.

Fancy dress party at Cosgrove Hall, 1946. Robin Winterbottom, in the sailor suit, is standing next to Frances Sweeny, daughter of Margaret Sweeny, later Margaret Duchess of Argyll

10
Pauline's secret son

ALTHOUGH GOOGLING 'PAULINE Sismey' did not yield anything except for a date of death, when I googled 'Pauline Dennistoun-Sword' I found the following entry in *The London Gazette*:

NOTICE is hereby given that by a deed poll dated the 28th day of October 1946 and duly enrolled in the Supreme court of Judicature on the 9th day of December 1946 JOHN HENRY REGINALD WINTERBOTTOM of Cosgrove Hall Stony Stratford in the county of Buckingham an infant and natural born British subject (acting by Pauline Vincent Dennistoun Sword his legal guardian) abandoned his former name of Daubeny and adopted the name of Winterbottom. LAURENCE COLLINS and FEARNLEY WHITTINGSTALL, 52, Lincoln's Inn Fields, W.C. Solicitors for the said John Henry Reginald Winterbottom.

The Winterbottoms, I discovered, had been a manufacturing family in the North of England and as they became wealthier, moved South and sent their sons to public schools such as Eton. Their history is found in the book *A Winterbottom Family*, compiled by American genealogist Susan Dorey, a distant relative. I obtained a copy of this book and there was the crucial entry that enabled me to trace Pauline's son. A Robin Winterbottom is described in Susan's book as being adopted, and the biological son of Reginald J. Daubeny and Pauline Vincent

Daubeny. He had been adopted by George Harold Winterbottom and his wife Penelope.

George Winterbottom had been educated at Eton, where he developed polio. This not only meant that he walked with a limp but that he could not father children. His first wife Cecile Eykyn had divorced him because of this and he then married Penelope, who knew that he could never have children although she longed for a family of her own. In 1928, George had bought Cosgrove Hall, a stately home.

Although Cosgrove Hall is no more, it has a large website consisting mainly of newspaper cuttings and photographs. Among the reports were several entries for Master Robin Winterbottom and also photographs of him as a child. In one line-up, where a number of children are in fancy dress, Robin is in a sailor suit and next to him is Frances Sweeny, daughter of Margaret Sweeny, formerly Margaret Whigham, who was presented at court in 1930 in the same batch as the then Pauline Turner.

Margaret Sweeny, later the notorious Margaret Duchess of Argyll, was a frequent visitor to Cosgrove Hall and the website indicated that the Winterbottoms were great party givers, holding many social events at their home and also often hosting fêtes and fundraisers for local charities. Several of these were opened by Prince Nicholas Galitzine and a newspaper report for 1935 says that he spoke with 'scarcely a Russian accent' as he declared the fête open. In one photograph, he is shown throwing darts. Another photographic line-up shows Princess Elena Galitzine and behind her, in a large picture hat, is a young woman described as Mrs Pauline Daubeny.

It also seemed, from the newspaper reports, that the Winterbottoms frequently entertained foreign royalty, as there are other stories and pictures showing them with the Princess of Albania, and others.

In 1948, the Winterbottoms sold Cosgrove Hall, after over 20 years in residence, and the following year, George Winterbottom died, aged 59. This meant that Penelope brought up Robin as a single parent. She sent him to Eton, which is described in Susan Dorey's book as 'an English private school'. From her researches, Susan Dorey discovered

Prince Nicholas Galitzine playing darts at a Cosgrove Hall fête, 1935

that Robin was adopted almost immediately after birth, even though the name change by deed poll did not happen until 1946. It appears, though, that the adoption was informal, as there was no adoption certificate to be found.

It now seemed a good idea to get in touch with Susan Dorey and also Toby Horton, who was George Winterbottom's nephew. He was born Gavin Tobias Alexander Winterbottom, from George Winterbottom's father's second marriage, and had changed his name to Horton, in memory of Horton Hall, his family's ancestral home, by deed poll.

I started thinking that changing one's surname by deed poll was quite common with this family I was trying to research, but also the very many name changes (and perhaps some fictitious names) were making the task of tracking them down quite difficult. Maybe that was the intention.

A book by Maureen Williams, *Gone But Not Forgotten*, loaned to me by Toby Horton, revealed that when Penelope Winterbottom died in 1977, her nephew Toby Horton was named as her sole heir. Did Robin, as the adopted son, not inherit anything, then? One might wonder why a nephew would take precedence over a son, even if adopted, but when I asked Toby Horton about Robin, he said that his aunt Penelope had never mentioned him.

This was all beginning to sound very odd. It soon became clear, though, that Pauline had some very close connection with the Winterbottoms although neither Toby nor Susan could shed any light on why George and Penelope should have adopted Robin in the first place. During the 1930s, Pauline, Princess Elena and Prince Nicholas Galitzine and also Prince Yurka Galitzine were regular visitors to Cosgrove Hall, so they were clearly close, but for the moment we could not work out why Pauline—and presumably her husband— might agree to hand over their son to the couple.

The Winterbottoms were not young when they adopted John Henry Reginald Winterbottom, to whom they gave the additional first name of Robin. George was 49 (born in 1890) and Penelope was 56. But they were the ideal adoptive parents, and they lavished every ounce of love and affection on him, which makes it all the stranger that Penelope cut Robin out of her Will and did not leave him even so much as a pair of cuff-links.

From the start, George Winterbottom was determined that Robin should have the kind of elite education that had been expended on him, and to this end put Robin's name down for Scaitcliffe, the exclusive boys' prep school situated at Egham, Surrey, and which was a feeder school for Eton. It is not known whether Robin boarded at Scaitcliffe, although given that his home, Cosgrove Hall, was very near Egham, this seems unlikely, even though it was common practice in those days to send six-year-old boys to boarding school as they were considered to be in need of 'toughening up' and that the Spartan regime of cold showers, compulsory games and corporal punishment was not then seen as unkind or particularly traumatic for a boy's development. Anything that could be described as mollycoddling was frowned upon.

At Cosgrove Hall, Robin enjoyed the kind of childhood that was then standard for rich, privileged children. Many visitors came to the house as Penelope was a great entertainer, a talented singer, and she was always holding balls, parties and fundraising events. There were also live-in servants to do the menial work, so George and Penelope lived lives of complete leisure, comfortably cushioned by the large inheritance he had received from his father, who had died in 1934, leaving today's equivalent of £500 million. George Harold senior had become one of the richest men in the country; so much so that when he died, he merited an obituary in the *New York Times* as well as in English papers.

As neither of the Winterbottoms worked, they had plenty of time to entertain Robin and make sure he was happy. George was an enthusiastic amateur artist and in fact was known as 'Artist' within the family. George's father had originally wanted to go to art school himself but his own father had forced him to join the family book cloth business instead. This was perhaps just as well as George senior made a massive fortune from the family firm whereas he might have struggled to make it as an artist. George II, with no need to earn a living, could indulge his artistic tendencies and he was also an avid art collector. He had a financial interest in an art gallery as well. So Robin would have been brought up surrounded by art, music and culture generally, plus a lot of people.

There was also of course, cricket. Scaitcliffe and its rival prep school Sunningdale were always holding cricket matches against each other. Once again, it is not known whether Robin played in any of these matches but as Scaitcliffe and Sunningdale were both very small schools, it is highly likely. Robin's adoptive father had won several cups for cricket while at Scaitcliffe which are now in the possession of his nephew Toby Horton. This was, of course, before he was crippled by polio, the illness which was serious in the days before an effective vaccine was developed, and which was very often misdiagnosed or not diagnosed at all. Princess Margaret's husband Anthony Armstrong-Jones, later Lord Snowdon, also developed polio while at Eton and although not as crippled and incapacitated as George Winterbottom, who had to walk with callipers, similarly walked with a limp and ended his days in a wheelchair.

It is probably not an exaggeration to say that Robin probably had a far happier childhood with the Winterbottoms than he would have had either with Pauline Dennistoun-Sword or her first husband Reginald Daubeny, as neither would have been able to offer him a settled childhood or home. There is also the fact that Pauline would have had to bring him up for the first seven years of his life as a single parent and then he would have had to get used to an unknown stepfather returning from his POW camp. Reginald Daubeny also remarried fairly soon after his divorce, so if he had gained custody of his son there would have been an unknown stepmother to get used to. There is also the important aspect that at Stony Stratford, Robin would have been out of the way of German bombs during the war.

No secret was ever made of the fact that Robin was adopted although I wonder whether, in view of his surname not being changed until 1946, the original adoption was intended to be temporary, and then, by the time he was eight years old, George and Penelope had become so much his 'real' parents that there could be no question of returning him to either of his biological parents.

But as so often happens, there was a serpent slithering away in the paradise and getting ever closer. Not long after Robin's adoption had been formalised by the name change (although there was never an official adoption) George began to be seriously ill, in and out of hospital. In 1948, after 20 years at Cosgrove Hall, the Winterbottoms felt they could no longer manage such a large house and put it up for sale. The sale was, pretty much like all the doings of the Winterbottoms, reported in all the local papers and the family moved to much smaller and more manageable premises, Kingswood House, in Sunningdale.

Toby Horton commented:

Cosgrove was quite a big set up and after the Second World War, taxation was very high indeed. 'Artist' [George Winterbottom] had always lived well and may have spent capital to keep things going. He had also been a partner in an art gallery, which was unlikely to have made any money. So the sale of Cosgrove and the move to Sunningdale, would have been for the sake of his physical and financial health as he got older.

He had been educated in the Sunningdale and Windsor area, so it was a logical move for his final years with far less personal and financial stress.

The *Northampton Mercury* for Friday 21 January 1949 reported that there was an 'open air goodbye' for Mr and Mrs Winterbottom and Master Robin Winterbottom. All the villagers turned out to wish this much-loved couple health and happiness in their new home.

But after less than a year there, George Winterbottom died, aged 59, on 3 July 1949, at the Princess Christian Nursing Home in Windsor. In the local newspaper reports of his funeral, Robin, now aged 11, was named at George's son, not his adopted son. George's Will was very simple. He left a net estate amounting to £62,698 (£2.5 million today) with everything going to his wife Penelope. Robin was not mentioned and nor was any provision made for his upbringing, education and maintenance, although he knew he could rely on Penelope to continue to do her best for the boy.

The executors of George's Will were Penelope, George's brother Oscar Dunston Winterbottom and his lawyer, Anthony Trower. On looking at the Will, Toby Horton remarked: 'It's interesting to see one of the Trowers on the list, as they guarded his, and Penelope's interests with great determination. Oscar was George's full surviving brother.'

Alastair Winterbottom, Toby Horton's father, was George's half-brother from George senior's second marriage to Georgina McLeod. Although by many people's standards, two million is a lot of money, it is not a huge sum with which to run a stately home, and I would imagine that Anthony Trower, George's lawyer, advised the sale of Cosgrove and the move to a smaller home that would cost less to run. George, it seemed, had ripped through his fortune fast.

Penelope, now aged 67, had to bring up Robin as a single parent. He had been entered for Eton soon after birth and arrived there in 1951, when he was placed in Mr Williams' house. The writer Ferdinand Mount, who was an exact contemporary of Robin's at Eton and who had attended the rival prep school of Sunningdale, said:

'Fishy Williams' house was a dimmish house.' This does not suggest that Robin was one of the brightest boys in the school, unlike Ferdy Mount, who went on to be a successful author and was also Margaret Thatcher's speech writer.

The Eton College archivist confirmed that Robin was admitted to the school with the following information:

> Robin entered the school in September 1951. His house-masters were W.W. Williams and then G.I. Brown, with Williams and then G.I. Bolton as his tutors. His guardian's address is first recorded as Mrs Winterbottom, Cosgrove, Coopers Hill, Englefield Green. Later it is High Peak, Sunningdale. In 1954 he won the Hamilton Divinity Prize. He left the school in July 1955 and the destination given was the RNVR.

On the list of new boys, Penelope is named as Robin's guardian but whether there was any legal process by which this came about is uncertain. Toby Horton said: 'Schools such as Eton were very used to irregular parentage and not too many awkward questions would be asked. If somebody called themselves a legal guardian, they would be accepted as such and no further investigations would be made. So long as the fees were paid, nobody much bothered, I imagine.'

It is interesting then, that Robin had two legal guardians and no actual mother! In the 1946 notice in *The London Gazette*, Pauline Dennistoun-Sword is named as her son's legal guardian and one may wonder why she was not named as the boy's mother. Another point is that although Robin's surname was not legally changed until he was eight years old, he was known as Robin Winterbottom in newspaper reports of Cosgrove Hall events long before this. It was a tangled heritage indeed, as according to Toby Horton, the Winterbottoms were extremely traditional, conservative people, not wild and flighty like Pauline.

Robin remained under the care of Penelope until he was 18 years old, and then in 1956 he joined the Royal Navy Voluntary Reserve. It is most likely that this counted as National Service as, until 1960, all able-bodied young men had to sign up to one of the three Armed Forces for two years. After National Service, young men from such schools as Eton might go on to university, usually Oxford or Cambridge, but there are no university records to be found for Robin.

In 1958, the RNVR, which attracted mainly the officer class, merged with the Royal Naval Reserve (RNR) but during the time they were separate units, the RNVR was considered the 'superior' reserve unit, for posh boys.

Susan Dorey managed to trace Robin through Army records until about 1962, when he had the rank of Lieutenant, and then the trail went cold. It became impossible to track him through Ancestry or other websites especially as there were a number of Robin Winterbottoms listed, and we could not be sure which, if any, was 'our' Robin. Susan found a marriage record for a Robin Winterbottom for 1959 and although this might have been possible, it didn't feel right, as I was pretty certain that Pauline had mentioned to my mother that her son was getting engaged, in 1962-ish.

Owing to our failure to find Robin Winterbottom online, we wondered whether he might have reverted to his original name of John, or even to his original surname, Daubeny. 'Robin Winterbottom' was, after all, a made-up name. But although searches revealed a John Winterbottom and also a John Daubeny, in Australia, neither seemed to be the man we were looking for.

But then Catherine Horwood-Barwise came to our rescue. By doing a DNA test, she discovered that she was related to Robin Winterbottom, of whom she had previously never heard, and that he was a 'first half-cousin'. She had found some interesting information about him and passed it on to me. It concerned the 'lovely girl' who Pauline had mentioned to my mother.

On 14 August 1963, the following announcement appeared in the Forthcoming Marriages section of *The Times*:

MR R. WINTERBOTTOM AND MISS A.E. HUDSON

The engagement is announced between Robin Winterbottom, of Gracious

Pond, Chobham, Surrey, and Ann, only daughter of Dr and Mrs H.G. Hudson, of Stanfield Hall, Wymondham, Norfolk.

At first, this announcement may sound innocent enough, much like any other engagement notice. But looking at it a little more closely, some anomalies immediately become apparent. It is usual, or was in those days, for the parentage of both parties to be given but here, only Ann's parents are named. As it happened Gracious Pond was Penelope Winterbottom's current address. She had moved there after selling the Sunningdale house, once again to cut costs as her capital was running out fast.

Robin, it seems, now aged 25, was living with her. The announcement appeared about a year after he appeared to have left the Royal Naval Voluntary Reserve, now the RNR of course. In joining the RNVR in the first place, Robin may have been influenced by his adoptive uncle Billy Winterbottom, who had joined the Reserve in the Second World War, and as Billy was one of the more dashing of the Winterbottoms, it may have seemed to Robin that to be a member of the RNVR, or the Wavy Navy as it was called, was a romantic thing to do.

Billy Winterbottom, who had also been educated at Eton as were most of the male Winterbottoms, had married Denise Lynch in 1933 after she divorced the notorious prankster Horace de Vere Cole. Horace's sister married Neville Chamberlain, the pre-war prime minister, although what Chamberlain thought of Horace as a brother-in-law has not been recorded. Billy Winterbottom qualified as a pilot in 1946 but died just a year later.

The records for Robin's naval career are patchy and inconclusive but there are a few details. In 1957 he was listed as a temporary midshipman and in January 1959 as an Acting Sub-Lieutenant. By spring 1962 he was listed as a Lieutenant and there the records end.

He did not make a career in the Armed Forces, but became a farmer, no doubt also a romantic notion possibly influenced by visits to his mother Pauline Sismey, who was living in the middle of farming country and who by 1963 had established a successful market garden business at Offord Cluny Manor. While Robin was learning the agricultural ropes in Norfolk, working with Dr Hudson on his ever-expanding farm, he met the 20-year-old Ann Hudson and they fell in love.

Note: I have since discovered that Robin went to Cirencester Agricultural College, now the Royal Agricultural University, where he trained as a farmer. This does not suggest any major academic ability, which is probably why, according to Ferdinand Mount, Robin was placed in a 'dimmish' house at Eton. In those days, the Cirencester College only accepted the cream—i.e., you had to be rich and thick to go there. Times have changed!

Six months after the engagement announcement, on 30 January 1964, a most peculiar notice appeared in a prominent position in *The Times* Court Circular:

Lieutenant-Colonel and Mrs O.N.D. Sismey leave for The Lebanon today. No letters will be forwarded. Mrs Sismey will be represented at the marriage of her son Mr Robin Winterbottom, on February 8, at Wymondham, Norfolk, by her brother Prince Yurka Galitzine.

Ever since 1803, it has been the practice of the Royal Household or 'Court' to circulate reports on the official daily engagements of the sovereign and other significant people. These notices are published in *The Times*, the *Telegraph* and the *Scotsman*, and since 2015, on Facebook.

It was true, especially in the days when the Court Circular carried many more announcements than it does today, that you had to be important, or deemed important, to merit an entry and at the very least to have a title. The mention of Prince Yurka would satisfy the title requirement and the notice bears the necessary dignified and sedate tone but otherwise, what is its point? Would anybody reading the Circular be remotely interested in where an obscure Colonel and his Lady were going on this day? Unless, of course, the notice was written in code and carried a specific meeting to those in the know.

Royal writer Anna Pasternak, author, amongst other books, of *Princess in Love*, a biography of Princess Diana, has said that the Court

Circular contains 'gems': hidden meanings which are buried beneath the apparent official tone of the notices. Although gossip columnists avidly scrutinise the Court Circulars in search of these gems, they certainly missed this one. Otherwise they might have unearthed a very strange story indeed.

An eagle-eyed gossip writer might have wondered, firstly, why Mrs Sismey was not named as Robin Winterbottom's mother on the engagement announcement, since she described herself as such in the Court Circular notice six months later. Also, as her son had a different surname, it would appear that Colonel Sismey was not the boy's father.

The wording of this particular announcement was, presumably, meant to convey an unavoidable diplomatic assignment for Colonel Sismey and it was standard for the wives of prominent men to accompany them on such missions. But was the date for their visit to Lebanon so crucial that it could not be put back eight days, or forward a couple of weeks to enable them to attend the wedding? Was there some kind of problem in Lebanon that necessitated the Sismeys' urgent attendance?

Looking at the history of Lebanon for those dates, there seemed no particular reason for them to be travelling there, and the Court Circular notice gives no reason for this visit. Colonel Sismey had long retired from the Army and there is no record of him ever having any diplomatic or official position. If the Sismeys were merely going on holiday, there would hardly be any point in including this in the Court Circular. But to announce a visit to Lebanon without giving a reason, sounded as if it might be a top-secret mission, which was probably the idea.

My own conclusion is that this announcement was put in as a face-saving operation to avoid embarrassment at the wedding and that in all likelihood, the Sismeys did not go to Lebanon, but remained holed up at Offord Cluny Manor instead. Robin's wedding certificate gives some credence to this possibility.

On the wedding certificate, the bride is named as Ann Elizabeth

Hudson, aged 21, a spinster living at Stanfield Hall, Wymondham, Norfolk. Her occupation is given as secretary. Her father is named as Dr Harold Hudson, a doctor and a farmer. Robin Winterbottom is described as being aged 26, a bachelor and a farmer. His address on the certificate is, once more, given as Gracious Pond, Chobham, Surrey.

This in itself is strange as Toby Horton, then still known as Gavin Winterbottom, and his family, became very friendly with Penelope during the 1960s, and Toby said that she never, ever, mentioned Robin. He said:

> I never met Robin who, as you know, had really been written out of the script by my Aunt Penelope's solicitor Tony Trower, and perhaps also my own family's solicitors had advised her not to include Robin in her Will.

> They were all extremely cautious lawyers who would have avoided the world of Pauline and the Daubenys like the plague. One of their tasks had always been to avoid predators, as Pauline's family would definitely have been seen!

And yet, although Toby never met him, Robin's home address is given as Penelope's in 1964. But Robin's Gracious Pond address is far from being the only oddity on the marriage certificate. If we look at the entry for Robin's father, he is named as Reginald Ernest Daubeny. The two witnesses to the wedding were Doreen Hudson, the bride's mother, and John Daubeny. Reginald was usually known as John. So why was he named as the father and not George Winterbottom, especially as Robin was named as George's son, not his adopted son, at his funeral? At the time of his marriage Robin was, it seemed, in the peculiar position of having two fathers and two mothers, with three parents still living.

One wonders what the very upright Dr Harold Hudson thought of all these ramifications!

I imagine that the Sismeys diplomatically absented themselves, as their presence might have caused some embarrassment at the wedding, and that Prince Yurka, who was by now a successful PR executive, made a suitable and suave substitute. The naming of Robin's father as Reginald Daubeny gives further ballast to Toby Horton's belief that the adoption was never formalised as, if it had been, the biological parents would have had to give up any claims on the child and would have forfeited parental rights. Indeed, until 1976, it was not possible for adoptees to contact their birth parents or source their original birth certificate and there is no substitute birth certificate for Robin in existence.

There was at the time a phrase, 'lawful children', by which is meant children of a properly conducted marriage. In order to become 'lawful' the pretence was maintained that adopted children were biological children.

It seems most likely, from Pauline Sismey and Reginald Daubeny being named publicly as Robin's parents, that Toby Horton is correct, and that Penelope's lawyers took fright and feared that the Daubenys and Sismeys might muscle in and even claim some of Penelope's money for themselves. They were certainly closing in as Robin's true parents, and Penelope, now aged 81, was being shoved out.

After the wedding, the happy couple lived at Manor Farm, Wymondham, very near to Ann's family, and the farm was their wedding present from Ann's wealthy parents. Manor Farm, about two miles from Stanfield Hall, dated back to the 17th century and was a mellow redbrick house of two storeys with five bedrooms, four bathrooms and three reception rooms. It also stood in grounds of 3.5 acres, so all in all it was not a bad place for the young couple to embark on married life. Ann loved horses and there was plenty of stabling for her to indulge her passion.

As well as being a doctor and a farmer, Ann's father Harold Hudson was also a historian and wrote several books on local history. His book, *Stanfield Hall*, explains the manor house's peculiar and sinister past. It is a large country house apparently built in the nineteenth century but according to Dr Hudson, its origins go back to at least the fourteenth century and the outside is just the façade to a much older building.

In 1848, Stanfield Hall was occupied by Isaac Jermy and his family, consisting at the time of his son, his son's wife and their infant daughter. A James Rush, who was a tenant farmer with nine children and, apparently, a violent and disagreeable man, had leased a couple of farms from the Jermy family. When he could not pay rent he decided to shoot them all dead and lay the blame on an illiterate jobbing gardener, Thomas Jermy, who thought he had some claim on the estate as he had the same unusual name as the owners.

On 28 November 1848, Rush, disguised in a wig and cloak, entered the Hall and shot dead Isaac Jermy, his son also called Isaac and wounded Isaac Junior's wife Sophia. A servant was also killed. Rush was arrested next day and brought to the local Assizes in March 1849, where he conducted his own defence. The jury took just ten minutes to find him guilty and he was hanged outside Norwich Castle on April 21, 1849, before a crowd estimated at 30,000. The case appears in many accounts of famous trials, and Dr Hudson writes in his book that, not surprisingly, after the three murders, nobody wanted to live in the Hall. Stanfield Hall has gone down in history as the scene of a particularly grisly triple murder, and retains its reputation to this day, still attracting sightseers.

In real life, the daughter of Sophia and Isaac junior later married into the local Gwyn family, who inherited the estate but never lived there. Instead, they rented it out to a series of farmers, and then sold it in 1921 to a George Rackham. Dr Hudson bought the estate in 1947 when it was in a very run-down condition, with the intention of turning it back into a family home. 'It became the focal point of my expanding farming business,' he wrote in his book, and added:

My wife and I were determined to nurse it back into good condition. She was an enthusiastic wall-paperer and painter. Every harvest when I was slaving on the combine, she, helped out by our odd job man Bert Lacey, would retrieve yet another room from its dingy condition. It took us 25 years to get the house ship-shape. By the time we left it was in excellent condition, and this heritage of the past should now be safe for many years.

The estate was sold in 1983 to a Simon Stearn, a farmer who once again used it for a family home. Dr Hudson was afraid it might be turned into a hotel or nursing home and 'would cease to be the family home that it had been for such a long time.' So far, his fears have been unfounded.

So Robin had married into a rich family who lived in a large country house, maybe with a background which was not all that different from that of the Winterbottoms, and Dr Hudson must have thought that Robin, with his Eton education and upbringing in a stately home, plus the fact that his mother now lived in a country mansion herself, was a reasonable match for his only daughter.

Now all that Robin had to do was to get down to the exacting tasks of being a hands-on farmer, husband and father. A year after the wedding, in February 1965, their daughter Sara was born at Aylesbury and on 17 January 1967 their son Mark James arrived at West Norwich Hospital. On Mark's birth certificate Robin's occupation is once again given as farmer, and the family address as Manor Farm, Wymondham.

Yet they were not a happy couple for very long. Two years after Mark's birth, Ann filed for divorce.

On 9 July 1970 the Decree Nisi was issued with Ann as Petitioner and Robin as Respondent. No Co-Respondent was named. The Decree Absolute was issued on 12 October 1970 and the marriage, solemnised on 8 February 1964, was legally dissolved. It had lasted just six years.

What went wrong? No grounds were given in the divorce papers but Manor Farm was sold and Ann moved back, now with two children, to Stanfield Hall. Robin fled away as far as he could. He ended up in Aberdeen where he bought a small bungalow and carried on working as a farmer.

Why Aberdeen? Susan Dorey says: 'One of the things I find curious is that at the end of his life Robin was living in Ellon, Scotland. This is 27 miles north of Stonehaven, Kincardineshire, where the Park family lived. They had a business, family and social relationship with the Winterbottoms. George Harold Winterbottom Senior was an executor of the estate of William Alexander Park, who lived from 1815 to 1889.'

It could be that Robin went to Aberdeen because of Winterbottom family connections, but it seems that by 1970 all communication between Penelope and Robin had been cut off. So it is more likely that he just wanted to start afresh, in a completely new area and where nobody knew him.

Whatever the reasons, he too, like his mother, became a bolter.

II

Back to Pauline

PAULINE REMAINED FRIENDLY with my mother and even gave me a wedding present when I married in August 1965. It came with a card bearing the scrawled message, 'To wish you very happy.'

Things were not going so well in the shop, however. Under incessant bullying from my brother, my mother decided to take him in the shop as an assistant, as he had not been able to hold down even the merest job in St Neots. She had hoped that he might join the navy as a boy entrant, given that he loved the water and had developed a passion for rowing. But he could not answer any of the questions on the very simple test paper and could not spell 'ocean'. As my mother said, 'the very thing he would be going on.'

Why did she do this? Perhaps guilt for never having wanted him and for the fact that he turned out a dud. One of my school friends said, perhaps unkindly but accurately, 'He was somebody who should never have been born.' But Mum refused to see this, and like many people with mentally deficient children, refused to see him that way, even though he could barely read and write. She had some inklings of his severe deficiencies but kept overriding them in the way that people often have, telling themselves that if you treat an abnormal person as normal, they will then become normal. This is rather like telling yourself that if you treat a dog as a cat, it will become a cat.

When Richard passed his driving test first time, she said: 'There are some things that they can do', knowing that his skill set was not very high and indeed, apart from his prowess at rowing, was pretty much non-existent.

Mum's customers were, though, all optimistic and Pauline said, 'It will be the making of him.' Unfortunately, this did not turn out to be the case. Richard was lazy, he often did not turn up to work: he wanted a free ride whereby he would get some money and spend all his time rowing. He had also married a couple of years after me, at 21. His bride was Lesley Bacchus, a Bedford girl who brought a dowry to the marriage. Her uncle, David Robinson, had founded Radio Rentals, from which he made an absolute fortune, and he settled a small private income on Lesley as well as buying her a mortgage-free house. Later, David Robinson founded Robinson College, Cambridge.

That marriage, not surprisingly, soon ran into difficulties and Lesley divorced him, running away, rather like Robin Winterbottom, as far as she could. The marriage produced two children, Samantha and Sean, who both turned out well. But Mum's shop assistants could not stand Richard, and soon left; Thelma to start her own shop in Godmanchester, which became so successful that it eventually kept three families.

Pauline continued to take a slight interest in me and often asked Mum what I was doing now as it was clear that I would never return to live in St Neots. Mum was able to reply with some pride, 'She's a journalist on local newspapers in Newcastle' and later, 'She's working at the *Sunday People*.'

'That rag!' exclaimed Pauline who, in common with many upper-class people of the day, took every single one of the Sunday papers. 'That rag' was at the time selling more than five million copies a week. 'What on earth is she doing on a scandal sheet like that? I would have thought that with her education, she would be on *The Times*.' Mum did not understand the world of newspapers and Fleet Street any more than Pauline did, and replied: 'Her husband is on *The Times*.' Of course I did not know at the time that Pauline herself had been in every newspaper of the day, in 1939. She never mentioned a word of this to anybody, so far as I knew.

Although Pauline continued working—or at least employing local workers—at her market gardening business, her drinking was now becoming serious and she was rarely sober. When Mrs Overton, Mum's driver until Richard's presence sent her away as well, went to Offord Cluny Manor to pick up deliveries, she often came back to report that Pauline was ill in bed. It was all rather like 'Jeffrey Bernard is Unwell' when the famous journalist was too 'ill'—for which read, too drunk—to write his weekly *Spectator* column.

Mrs Overton used to say, 'I hear she's been at the gin bottle again.' And now, when Pauline came into the shop, she often slurred her words and was frequently incoherent. The gossip mill went into over-drive and now, when those customers who knew Pauline came into the shop, asked: 'Is she ever sober these days?'

Pauline Sismey was not the only drunkard Mum had to deal with. She humoured Pauline whenever she came into the shop—still parking her car in the middle of the road—but closer to home, Dad had turned into a drunkard. He had an accident of some kind at work for which he got some financial compensation and took early retire-ment. Now, he spent his days sitting in a chair with a bottle of gin or whisky beside him. This led to his early death and on his death certificate, under 'cause of death' was 'chronic alcohol abuse'.

It was as if Mum had to have some horrible male in her life and felt bereft without one. Richard stuck to her like a limpet, even living back at home when his marriage to Lesley ended.

Pauline, in spite of her levels of drinking and smoking, lived on until 1980. She was aged 68 when she died and had been ill for some years. On her death certificate, the causes of death were given as: Bronchopneumonia, 2, congestive cardiac failure, 3, ischaemic heart disease and 4, chronic obstructive airway disease. Nowhere on the certificate is 'chronic alcohol abuse' mentioned. Instead, euphe-misms were employed, which goes to show that death certificates are not always any more reliably accurate than the other certificates issued for important rites of passage such as being born or getting married.

The informant on Pauline's death was her husband and she died at their home. Her 'occupation' on the death certificate was given as 'Wife of Lt. Col. Oliver North Deane Sismey, Army Officer (retired)'. There was no mention that for many years she had not only run a market garden but had opened the decorative gardens to the public and played a huge part in local flower and gardening societies. Turner is given for her maiden name, date and place of birth 17 March 1912, France.

Although Oliver's posh neighbours were initially scandalised when he married the 'flighty' Pauline, it has to be remembered that, in effect, he had not been married before. His very young first wife left him after only a couple of years and until his mid-50s he had never experienced what might be called a normal married life, however that might be defined. Pauline breathed life and energy into the tired old Manor, enlivened it with her dinner parties, her socializing and the constant stream of customers who arrived to pick up their orders of fruit or veg. She also breathed new life into the tired old Colonel who had been quietly mouldering away becoming prematurely aged.

She involved many of the villagers in her business, and so became an employer. In fact, we had come to think of her, rather than Oliver, as the owner of the Manor. My mother said: 'I think the Colonel just does what she tells him. She seems to be the boss there.' Oliver was shuffling in the background and obeying orders, for all that he had commanded crack units during the war. Perhaps Pauline remained the unit that he was unable to crack. He was 80 when she died and was to live on for another 13 years.

Pauline left a Will, dated 30 October 1979, the year before she died, which sheds more light on her family, although not on her origins. There were some minor bequests to local people who had helped with her market garden. The mink coat, once stolen by Victor Hervey and draped round her shoulders when shopping in St Neots, was bequeathed to her husband's daughter Islay Edwards. There was also an ermine coat which was left to a friend named Patience Lambert.

The main beneficiary is her son, John Henry Reginald Winterbottom (hereinafter known as 'Robin Winterbottom'). To him she leaves her silver, which after his death goes to the sons of his second marriage to Jean Winterbottom (née Robertson) in equal shares. She adds that the silver may be inspected from time to time by her executors Judy Sophia Lane and Peregrine Edward Lort-Phillips, plus a local solicitor. The silver is to be insured and kept in good repair at Robin's expense.

The children of Robin's first marriage, Sara and Mark, are also mentioned, and Pauline's chattels are to be divided equally between the four grandchildren. So far as the actual money is concerned, most of this—around £30,000 (£200,000 today)—goes to her husband Oliver Sismey.

And now here is the interesting bit:

I give devise and bequeath all the property comprised in the Princess Pauline Galitzine Settlement administered by the Public Trustee under numbers (listed) over which I have a general testamentary power of appointment unto my Trustees to sell call in and convert the same into money ... and I direct my Trustees to invest the same funds for my said grandchildren Paul Shaun Winterbottom and Johnathan Rory Winterbottom as they attain the age of 25 years in equal shares absolutely.

When I contacted the Public Trustee's office to enquire about this Settlement, I was told that Settlements were not in the public domain and only direct beneficiaries could have access to the records. This 'Settlement' would have been distinct from the other assets listed in the Will, and as such, administered separately.

The Will goes on to say that she desires to be buried beside her husband, still alive at this point, in Offord Cluny churchyard, and that a memorial tablet be erected in her memory near to the Sismey family pew in Offord Cluny church, the costs to be borne by her residuary estate.

Now that I had more details about Pauline's grandchildren, it might be possible to trace them. Most online searches threw up the famous name of film director Michael Winterbottom and so far as I knew, he was not related to 'our' Winterbottoms. Sara Winterbottom proved elusive and as for Mark Winterbottom, there were several on Google and there was no way of knowing which might be the right one. Similarly there were several Paul Winterbottoms, but I thought I might have more luck with the youngest grandchild, as the spelling of 'Johnathan' was unusual.

Yes, there he was, Johnathan Rory Winterbottom. I discovered that he lived in Aberdeen, was a financial consultant and married to Cheree Winterbottom. He had two small children. Cheree Winterbottom has a Facebook account showing photos of them at their wedding, with Johnny dressed in a Gordon Highlanders' kilt. Had he known, then, about his step-grandfather Colin Dennistoun-Sword, of the 1st Battalion Gordon Highlanders? The Gordon Highlanders' Museum, containing Colin's war records, is of course in Aberdeen. Johnny's business, Target Financial Planning, also came up on company records, listing him and Cheree as directors.

The name Jean Winterbottom also came up on searches and I discovered she had died in 2017, aged 66, and had been the beloved wife of Robin Winterbottom who had died in 2009.

Yes, this was 'our' family without doubt. I was able to write to Johnny Winterbottom who initially said he would be delighted to help me and that his brother Paul had a suitcase in his garage full of Robin's documents which did not mean a lot to him. However, further emails elicited no reply and although I had hoped to be able to go through that suitcase, at the time of writing that has not happened. I think that Paul was nervous although Johnny told me that Sara had passed away in 2013 and that Mark Winterbottom lived in London and was an executive with BSkyB. I wrote to him but did not get a reply.

Several other people I contacted who would have known Robin either did not respond at all or informed me in a curt email that they were unable to help.

Scottish marriage certificates give much more information than their English equivalents, and for Robin Winterbottom, occupation once again given as farmer, there are the following details: in the space for Bridegroom is the name Winterbottom and in brackets, formerly Daubeny, and in the space for first name is Robin and once again, in brackets, it says, formerly John Henry Reginald. Robin's marital status is given as divorced and his birthplace as London.

Robin's father is named as Reginald Ernest John Daubeny, occupation Company Director (Finance) and his mother as Pauline Vincent Daubeny, afterwards Dennistoun-Sword, now Sismey.

Robin's second bride was named as Jean Robertson, a student teacher. Her marital status is given as spinster and her date of birth, 14 December 1950, making her 12 years Robin's junior. She was a local girl, hailing from Torpins, a village just outside Aberdeen. Her father Douglas Robertson was also described as a farmer. The date of the wedding was 30 June 1972, less than two years after his divorce from Ann was made absolute. There is no indication that Jean was the co-respondent in the divorce as he did not meet her until he moved up to Aberdeen.

On moving to Scotland, Robin had bought Overton House, a small one-storey cottage situated in Ellon, a suburb of Aberdeen. Not of particularly high value and certainly not what he was used to, it was sold in 2004 for £170,000. But possibly, it was all he could afford after the divorce.

It seems, from the details on the certificate, that Robin and Jean were married at Robin's home and that the ceremony was performed by the Rev G.W. Gregory, the Congregational Minister of Trinity Congregational Church, Aberdeen. Once again, Robin would not then have been allowed to marry in church as a divorcee, but in some cases dissenting ministers would agree to bless the wedding, which is what appears to have happened here. Usually, nonconformist ministers would only agree to bless a second wedding if they were convinced that the divorcee was the innocent party. The days of 'innocent' and 'guilty' parties are long over but it was bold of Ann to sue for divorce after such a short marriage and with two small children. There must have been some strong grounds to satisfy the courts, but they do not appear on the Decree Absolute.

The certificate to legalise Robin's second marriage was also signed by the local registrar. Robin retained the name Winterbottom, while acknowledging a change of surname and first names on the certificate.

The reason for the additional information on Scottish marriage certificates was that many English people ran away to Scotland to be married, and the Scottish authorities wanted to be certain that the marriage in question was a 'regular' one and that each of the parties was free to marry. Knowing that people often changed their names when eloping to Scotland, they also wanted to be sure that the people getting married were who they said they were. Therefore, Robin would have been asked about any change of name and about both of his parents, as on English certificates only the father was named.

Although Pauline did not attend Robin's first wedding, probably because of Penelope Winterbottom and her first husband John Daubeny being there, I discovered at a late stage that she DID attend this second wedding and made a great fuss about doing so. For more details, see the Appendix at the end of the book.

After the trauma of his divorce and flight to Aberdeen, it had not taken long for Robin to find a second wife. This time the marriage lasted and in 1975 their first son Paul was born, followed in 1977 by Johnathan.

That same year, 1977, his adoptive mother Penelope Winterbottom died, aged 94. She had made her last Will and Testament on 3 October 1972, where she appointed Anthony Trower of Trower, Still and Keeling as her sole executor. In a codicil for 26 January 1977 she says 'I give, devise and bequeath all my real and personal property not otherwise disposed of to my nephew G.T.A (Toby) Winterbottom'. Penelope's signature is very shaky at this point and the codicil was very probably written for her by Anthony Trower. This was probably done to make doubly sure that Robin, now with four children, did not get his hands on any vestige of her estate, or contest her Will.

In her original Will, it is surprising that Penelope does not mention Robin at all, as she leaves small sums and objects to various friends and neighbours. By the time she died though, she did not have a great deal of money to leave as the net value of her estate only amounted to £20,379. But Wills can be peculiar things, which is why they were so often the subject of family disputes in Victorian novels and indeed, still are. Toby Horton said: 'Trower was determined to see Robin written out of the script for reasons known only to him.' This determination may be why Trower was not only present at the writing of the later codicil but even wrote it himself with Penelope looking on. He may have wanted to be absolutely certain that she did not write Robin back in.

Once he moved to Aberdeen, Robin was never again to live in a stately home and nor was he to send his own sons to Eton. Instead they went to local state schools while Robin became a pillar of the local community. He was chairman of the local community council and, according to reports in the *Aberdeen Press and Journal*, was very vocal on conservation and planning issues.

After becoming parents, Robin and Jean moved to a larger house, Coalmoss Croft, Ythanbank, Ellon, a detached former croft. There Robin carried on for a time his profession of farmer, although Coalmoss was more of a smallholding than an actual farm. It was certainly not on the same scale as his former father-in-law Dr Harold Hudson's farm. Now, after being brought up in a stately home, sent to possibly the most famous school in the world and marrying into a rich farmer's family, Robin's life became very modest. Maybe one reason for this was that he had started to become ill from the condition that would eventually kill him, multiple sclerosis. This started to affect his movements so much that he could no longer carry on with farming and he had to find another job. He became a Fire Protection Officer and one Ellon resident remembers him walking with a stick and after that giving up the smallholding and selling fire extinguishers, although he continued to live at Coalmoss Croft.

Robin died on 13 September 2009, at 11.30 hours at Auchtercrag House, an Aberdeen nursing home. He was 71 years old and the fees at Auchtercrag were £1000 a week. On its website, the care home is licensed for looking after those with physical disability. Once again, Robin's death certificate is far more detailed than its English equivalent would be.

In the space for forenames is Robin (formerly John Henry Reginald) and in the space for surname is: Winterbottom (formerly Daubeny). Robin's occupation was given as Fire Protection Consultant (Retired) and his home address as Coalmoss Croft.

In the space for forenames and occupation of spouse(s) or civil partners was given:

Anne Hudson

Jean Robertson

Jean's occupation is given as Nursing Team Leader, a job she trained for after having children.

Robin's father was once again named as Reginald Ernest John Daubeny, Company Finance Director (deceased) and his mother, Pauline Vincent Turner or Daubeny or Dennistoun-Sword or Sismey (deceased). No occupation was given for Pauline. Reginald Daubeny had died in 1995, aged 86.

The certificate was signed by Jean Winterbottom, named as widow. A year after Robin's death Coalmoss Croft was sold for £260,000.

By this time however, Jean herself was far from well and she died in 2017 aged 66, also from multiple sclerosis.

The following notice appeared in the *Aberdeen Press and Journal*:

WINTERBOTTOM (ALFORD/ELLON) Suddenly but peacefully at Aberdeen Royal Infirmary, on Sunday March 12, 2017, Jean Winterbottom, aged 66 years. Much loved wife of the late Robin, dearly loved mother of Paul and Johnathan and friend to many. Service at St. Mary on the Rock, Ellon, on Thursday March 23, at 11.30am, thereafter to Ellon Cemetery. All friends respectfully invited. Family flowers only please. Donations if desired at the church for M.S. Society.

Jean, like Robin, had also played a large part in community affairs, organizing fundraising events, and she was a stalwart member of the Women's Institute.

So what can we say about Robin's life? Was it a kind of hurry on down, going from an upbringing in a huge country house, meeting foreign royalty and other dignitaries as a matter of course, an elite education, a commission in the RNVR, to end up with a job as a Fire Protection Consultant and living in a modest former croft? How much did his rather sad adult life have to do with having a bolter as a mother?

The author Rory Knight Bruce, whose mother was another bolter, reckons that her flight from his father, when Rory was two years old, traumatised him for life. His mother, television presenter Gwynneth Tighe, told people that she fled from a monster, to which the answer was: 'You left your children with a monster?'

Robin's adoptive parents were not monsters, far from it, but we have no record about what he thought when, in later life, his actual parents reclaimed him. Was it their reappearance in Robin's life that persuaded Penelope to cut him out of her Will? And as to being mysterious, Toby Horton said that she never mentioned Robin and in fact, until Susan Dorey wrote her magnum opus about the Winterbottom family, he had no information about Robin at all.

Similarly, in Huntingdonshire, although Pauline was a well-known local figure, none of her friends, neighbours or colleagues even knew she had a son. The only reason I knew was because she had once or twice mentioned him to my mother, but perhaps she never breathed a word to anybody else. At least, none of the locals I questioned had any idea that there was a son in the background. Nobody had ever seen him and the only person who had any recollection of him was Rosemary Wolrige-Gordon, who had served with him on the local Ellon council. She, though, had no knowledge of his background.

Why did Pauline keep him such a secret? Why did he never visit her at The Red House, Waresley? We shall probably never know the answers, although Rory Knight Bruce's memoir gives some insight into the bolter mentality. Bolters, it seems, have an uncanny ability to shrug off the past and live for the present and future. Thus, both Pauline and Gwynneth Tighe shed husbands without so much as a backward glance, and they were able to shed their children with the same insouciance, or lack of sentimentality, however you like to see it.

There is perhaps some excuse for Gwynneth Tighe as she ambitiously pursued a television career when women were thin on the ground in this new medium, but Pauline never had a career to follow. The term 'bolter' originated in Nancy Mitford's *The Pursuit of Love*, and it seems that these bolters were always pursuing love, although they rarely found it. Nancy Mitford's bolter is based on the real-life bolter Idina Sackville, whose whole existence was based on chasing one man after another; very often unsuitable ones at that.

And what of Ann, Robin's first wife who is also named on his death certificate? She also disappeared from the scene. The last piece of information I could find about her was in 1972, when she was back living at her parents' house. In 2020, Catherine Horwood-Barwise, who was trying to complete her family tree, attempted to track her down but without success. I could get no leads either until I ordered a copy of her father Dr Harold Hudson's Will. As she was born in 1942 it was possible that she was still alive and, according to Catherine, 'What a story she would have to tell.'

Dr Hudson died in 1993 and was described as a retired farmer. After his first wife died, he married again and his executors were named as David Crawford O'Neill, a solicitor, his second wife Ruth Helen Hudson and his grandson Mark James Winterbottom, then aged 27. At the time of his death Dr Hudson was domiciled in Jersey, possibly for tax reasons as his home address is given as St Mary's, Wymondham, a substantial house with four bedrooms and two bathrooms.

Among other bequests, Dr Hudson left £30,000 to his daughter, named as Ann Elizabeth Gaunt Blum. £15,000 went to Sara Winterbottom, Robin's only daughter, along with some paintings, and another £15,000 went to Mark Winterbottom, as well as 'such motor car as I own after my death'. The house, St Mary's, went to his second wife Ruth plus the sum of £200,000. Dr Hudson's estate was valued at £909,873.

It appears from this Will that Ann had married again but there seemed to be no more children. I discovered that she was still alive and was living at a flat in Wimbledon, but as there was no Mr Blum listed, he had probably died. He was not mentioned in Dr Hudson's Will, so there may have been another divorce. I wrote to Ann but did not get a reply so once again, had to assume she did not want to revisit those times.

At this stage there was still much that had not been revealed, such as who was his grandfather, as the Henry Stanley Turner named on Pauline's three marriage certificates did not seem to exist. His grandmother, Princess Elena Galitzine, certainly existed but her only grandson, at the time she wrote her Will, is not mentioned. Poor old Robin: it seems as though everybody did their best, including his mother, to wipe him out. After all, she had not attended his first wedding.

All of them would have a tale to tell so it is a pity that none of those still living have seen fit to tell it.

12

What about the brother?

ALTHOUGH PAULINE ONLY hit the headlines once, when she gave evidence at the Old Bailey in 1939, her half-brother Prince Yurka was much more of a public figure. He has been written up in several books, the latest being *An Unanchored Heart*, by Rory Knight Bruce, where he is constantly referred to as 'The Russian Prince'. Yurka was Rory's stepfather, as he was married to his mother, Irish television personality Gwynneth Tighe.

This is what Rory has to say about Prince Yurka:

> She had married a White Russian prince and converted to Russian orthodoxy. This man was charming, slow, softly spoken, resigned to his loss of status following the Russian Revolution. His family had been important and his grandfather had been the last Tsar's prime minister but now, having come to England with only the shirt on his back, he seemed resigned to a life spared and the simple social joys that London had to offer. He, too, had been married a couple of times before, with one son my age, Gregory, who had a pronounced limp… The papers were once again agog and I have pictures of the Prince and Princess from my mother's voluminous scrap album.

Rory's description, although romantic, is not quite accurate, as Yurka did not arrive in England 'with only the shirt on his back' but was born in 1919 in Yokohama, Japan, to Prince Nicholas Galitzine, who had ended up painting pub signs in and around Waresley, and Princess Elena Galitzine, the former Emma Lilian Fawcett-Hodgson, from Liverpool. There is no mention of Pauline in Rory's book and he said he had never met her.

Even if Rory's description was somewhat fanciful, it is true to say that Prince Yurka was a colourful character who exhibited much of his father's flamboyance, and then some. He was married four times in all, and each of his wives became Princesses on marriage. During her marriage to him, Gwynneth Tighe became known as Princess Elizabeth Galitzine. There were also four daughters from various marriages, who also became Princesses at birth.

There were six years between Pauline and Yurka and they had different fathers, but they were very close to each other throughout their lives. He was a witness at her third wedding to the Colonel, and also stood in for her when she absented herself from Robin's first wedding. There is, though, still something of a Russian mystery about Yurka, as nobody is quite sure what happened in his early years. Catherine Horwood-Barwise says that he was brought up at 28 Elm Tree Road, St John's Wood, and yet his obituary in the *Rutland Times* states that the first seven years of his life were spent in France and Austria and that his parents returned to England so that he could have an English education.

Certainly by 1927, when Yurka would have been about eight, his parents were living in London, where they remained until they took up residence in the Red House, Waresley, during the war. There is a news story in the *Biggleswade Chronicle* of Prince Nicholas giving a 'fascinating talk on Japan' at the town hall in 1943.

By the time war broke out Yurka was adult and independent, no longer living with his parents. In 1939 he was sharing a flat with Pauline when she was going through her first divorce. There is no information available for his early schooling but at the age of 12 he was sent to Stowe, a relatively new public school which Richard Branson's father (and Richard himself) also attended. Another mystery arises about what he did after leaving school. His obituary says that 'the money ran out' and instead of continuing at Stowe and perhaps going on to university, Yurka was apprenticed aged 16 to a glove-maker. This did not last and he was soon apprenticed to Fairey Aviation. Then, as with so many young men of the time, he joined the Army and was enlisted with the Middlesex Regiment.

In 1939, Yurka joined the Right Club along with Pauline and Colin Dennistoun-Sword. On unearthing *The Red Book*, which gave a list of the 235 members of the Club, author Robin Saikia decided to investigate him, and writes on his website, Foxley Books:

> The most remarkable story I unearthed while researching *The Red Book* was that of White Russian Prince Yuri Galitzine, known as 'Yurka' to his friends. The discovery of Yurka was one of those rare moments, a bright sunrise and I hope, worth sharing.

Saikia goes on to say that when he was researching *The Red Book*, the name of Yurka, listed as 'Turka Galitzine', stood out because it was a noticeably foreign name among the list of otherwise very English names. The name intrigued Saikia because nobody he contacted seemed to be able to identify this mysterious person. Then, he says, he came across a police report written by one of the infiltrators of the Right Club, naming a 'Eurha' at the Club meetings. After that it became relatively easy to track down the elusive Turka/Eurha and identify him as Yuri Galitzine. Saikia embarked on a quest to find out more about the young Russian prince and traced him to the Imperial War Museum in London where he found Yurka's very detailed war diaries. They were, adds Saikia, 'a meticulously compiled scrapbook of photographs, tickets, press cuttings, explanatory notes, reference to girlfriends—his own and other people's—and to cars, planes, trips, dances.'

Saikia discovered that the early part of the diaries was cheerful and optimistic but that the tone became distinctly darker as the war went on. Whenever friends or relatives were captured, reported missing or wounded, Yurka carefully cut out the stories from the newspapers and pasted them into his war diary. Thus, the report of his brother-in-law Colin Dennistoun-Sword's capture and imprisonment was included and Yurka also noted when fellow officers had been killed.

By 1944, according to Saikia, Yurka was at a great distance from the atmosphere of the Right Club cocktail parties in Kensington Square and the diaries darkened still further when he was seconded to the Political Warfare Department of the Supreme Headquarters Allied Expeditionary Forces. It was at this point, says Saikia, that his story became truly absorbing.

An American officer, Alfred de Garcia, also attached to SHAEF, remembered Yurka clearly: 'Captain Galitzine, handsome and humane, somehow detaches himself and even gets back to England to get married but then returns like an eel to the Sargasso Sea, much alive and smiling. He has smashing pictures of the High Society wedding and articles from the Press.'

By D-Day, Yurka was commanding the Propaganda Unit of the US 45th Division, which was involved in War Crimes Investigations. It was while he was engaged in this that he had his Damascene moment and completely changed his former Fascist, right-wing, pro-German views for ever.

He was sent to investigate Natzweiler, a concentration camp in France, and in an account given by Rita Kramer, author of *Flames in the Field*, the story of four SOE (Special Operations Executive) women, she describes Yurka as 'a twenty-one-year-old British officer, son of a White Russian father and an English mother'. In fact, Yurka was aged 25 by now. She goes on to say that Yurka carefully put together a record of 'the systematic shootings, hangings and gassings, the medical experiments carried out on live prisoners, the conditions of slave labour on starvation rations, the brutal punishments randomly inflicted by sadistic criminals put in charge of the barracks, and other details of daily life in the camps that had been intended to pave the way for the New Order promised by the Third Reich.'

She adds: 'No one would believe him.'
Yurka's own account reads thus:

The SS men conducting the interrogation were given wine and spirits to whip
up their fury still further and afterwards, knew no restraints. The prisoners
in the next room could not sleep during the night because of the continuous
cries of pain from those being tortured. At reveille, the accused were taken
away. Most of them had been tortured to such an extent that they were entirely
beyond recognition. After four weeks, during which they continued to have
their hands tied to their backs and were exposed to the weather, those concerned were publicly hung, in the presence of all the prisoners. Those chained
in this manner had remained chained at all times and their hands were not
free when they had to relieve themselves or to eat and drink. The chains grew
into their flesh, the upper arms were blue from the stopped blood and had (so
to speak) died off.

He went further. In the last weeks of the war, Yurka had plans for
an International Bureau of Information, where information about
the war would be shared, and the attempts by extremists for global
domination would be stopped. The idea was that this Bureau would
provide a weapon for peace. In a letter to *The Times* on 11 October 1945,
Yurka wrote:

Few people realise the part propaganda had played in this war and even in
the last war. It might well be said that Germany declared war on the world in
1935 when Hitler launched his propaganda offensive against civilization, and
it is certain that the measure of success he achieved was in the main due to
the influencing of public opinion, especially in undermining the unity of his
victims by propaganda.

Robin Saikia ended his account of Yurka's complete volte-face from
his earlier pro-German views by writing: 'Yurka, unlike many of
his fellow Right Club members, had travelled a long way since that
first club meeting in South Kensington in 1939.' Which all goes to

show, not everybody is beyond redemption and that sometimes fate reshapes us in the most dramatic and unexpected ways. 'Ironically,' Saikia wrote, 'Yurka forged a highly successful career as a PR tycoon in the 50s and 60s. He had the courage to change his mind. The rest of these men never changed their mind.'

I am not sure that it is entirely true that Yurka was the only former member of the Right Club to change his mind, as Pauline and Colin Dennistoun-Sword also dissociated themselves from their pre-war fascism, although I don't know how serious their conviction was in the first place. Colin of course had endured five years as a POW, so it was very unlikely that he would remain pro-Nazi or pro-fascist.

As it turned out, Robin Winterbottom was not the only Robin who was difficult to trace. In fact, it proved impossible to track down Robin Saikia, a half-Indian writer who until 2010 had a high profile in the media. And a copy of *The Red Book*, which was firstly on sale through Amazon at a price of £3,641.99, then became unavailable anywhere, at any price. Robin Saikia's website and email address no longer seemed to exist either. Foxley Books, his publishing company, also appears to have ceased business.

A further account of Yurka's war exploits is contained in Ben Macintyre's book *SAS Rogue Heroes*, where he writes of 'a Russian prince of royal blood.'

> Captain Prince Yuri Galitzine could trace his lineage back to the Grand Dukes of Lithuania, the royal family of Poland and the Tsars. With the Bolshevik Revolution, the Galitzine dynasty had seen harder times. After schooling in England, Galitzine himself had become a glove-maker and then an apprentice at an aircraft factory. During the war he served as a liaison officer to the Free French, and then in the Allied military propaganda unit, where he had witnessed Nazi barbarity at first hand as one of the first British soldiers to enter Natzweiler-Struthof concentration camp.

After the war, Major Eric 'Bill' Barkworth led a unit to track down Nazi criminals and Yurka was part of this unit. Yurka described the

Major as a 'mystic, a thinker' and when Barkworth suggested using a Ouija board to track down suspects, Yurka did not dismiss the idea out of hand. Instead, Macintyre writes: 'He became an enthusiastic supporter of this form of Nazi-hunting.' Ouija boards are used to communicate with the dead, and Barkworth, who was interested in spiritualism, said: 'If people were killed, presumably they will want to tell us what happened to them.'

This is the only reference to Yurka being interested in spiritualism or contacting the dead and is contained in Macintyre's book where he says that Barkworth had an 'otherworldly air' that appealed to 'the Russian's sense of magic'. Presumably Macintyre had at the back of his mind such Russian mystics as the 'mad monk' Rasputin and Helena Blavatsky, founder of the Theosophy movement, and maybe assumed that all Russians, including Yurka, had a trace of mysticism in their make-up. But of course, Yurka was only half-Russian, a detail Macintyre omits from his book. At any rate there is no further indication that Yurka was interested in spiritualism. Rather the reverse, I would have thought, as he became a hard-headed and very successful businessman.

However, not a single one of the accounts, including the latest by Rory Knight Bruce, misses drawing attention to his noble White Russian heritage, and a lot of the glamour surrounding him in adult life definitely came from this background. This was also played up during the 1939 reports of the theft of Pauline's jewellery and furs, although Pauline herself did not have a drop of royal Russian blood in her veins.

The marriage that Yurka hurried back to England to celebrate was to Constance Higginson, whom he had met when he was serving in Northern Ireland. The marriage took place on 22 November 1944 at St Columba's Church in Knightsbridge and produced one daughter, Alexandra. But it did not last and the couple were divorced in 1951 on the grounds of desertion by his wife since 1948.

Before the Decree Absolute came through, Yurka had a brief affair with Clothilde Ward, four years his senior, and this relationship produced Catherine, later Catherine Horwood-Barwise.

In 1952, just one year after his first divorce, Yurka married the American Sheilagh Sandford-Johnson, the only daughter of widower Colonel B. Sandford-Johnson. This marriage was solemnised at the Russian Orthodox Church in London and produced a son, Grigori, or Gregory, and a daughter, Sophia. It might be said here that not only was Yurka an assiduous Nazi hunter, he was a dedicated wife hunter as well.

This marriage did not last either and it was dissolved in 1964. The divorce attracted newspaper interest and there were pictures of Princess Sheilagh Galitzine striding out from the divorce court, wearing a big hat, white gloves, a sleeveless dress and court shoes.

After two marriages to relative nobodies, Yurka's third marriage was to a 'somebody'. In 1965 he married the glamorous Irish actress and TV presenter Gwynneth Tighe, who had appeared in The Saint in 1962. That marriage produced two children: Nicholas, and Amalia, who was born in 1970 and lived for only two days. She is buried in her grandparents' grave at Waresley.

Gwynneth Tighe had a son, Rory, from a previous marriage, who became known as the writer Rory Knight Bruce. In his memoir An Unanchored Heart, Rory describes how his mother, another bolter, abandoned him when he was one year old to pursue her television career, and to marry The Russian Prince, as Yurka is referred to in the book. Rory writes, however, that Yurka became like a second father to him, and has fond memories of him, although he never met Pauline or knew anything about her.

The marriage to Gwynneth Tighe was dissolved in 1976 on the grounds that the couple had not lived together for more than two years. It was duly reported in the Daily Mirror and that same year, Yurka embarked on matrimony yet again, this time to Dr Jean Shanks, a high-profile pathologist and very different from Gwynneth. This was by far his most successful marriage and lasted, although it did not produce any more children.

His life changed on his marriage to Jean Shanks, Oxford graduate and phenomenally successful businesswoman who in 1986 set up the

Jean Shanks pathology services. The following year JS Pathology was launched on the stock market and was employing a total of 274 staff handling around 2000 patients a day. At last, maybe, here was a marriage of equals and Yurka became a director of Dr Shanks' pathology business.

Yurka and Jean moved to Rutland in 1976 and as well as continuing to run his business from a London address, he had also become passionately interested in local history, helping to form the Rutland Local History Society and becoming its President. Here, perhaps, is an echo of his father Prince Nicholas's interest in English village life, when he lived in Waresley and became the de facto Lord of the Manor.

In 1982, the *Rutland Times* published a long interview with Prince Yurka. The background to the article states that Prince Yuri's father Prince Nicholas first came to England in 1916 as Assistant Military Attaché to the Russian Embassy in London, where he remained for two years. The article does not say that Nicholas was only 19 at the time, or that he was only 20 when he married Emma Hodgson Turner in 1918. However, it goes on to say that the newly-wed Galitzines went to America where Nicholas was on a trip to purchase munitions for the White Russian Army. Yuri made his appearance early, necessitating the stopover in Japan.

The article says that Prince Nicholas was in the Ukraine fighting the Bolsheviks in 1920. This was presumably the Ukrainian War of Independence, which lasted from 1917 to 1921 and resulted in the Ukraine being absorbed into Soviet Russia. This was the first I had heard of Nicholas's involvement in this war and the article adds that Yuri's mother Princess Elena had decided to move to Russia during this time.

After a short time, the article goes on to say, the Kroner crashed and the family moved to Paris. They arrived with three large trunks full of worthless money which Yuri's father, who had moved to Paris after his estates were stolen by the Bolsheviks, used to paper a room. The article once again says that Yuri and his parents only moved back to London when Yuri was seven years old so that he could have an

English education. There is no mention made in the article of an older sister and one assumes from the interview that Yuri is an only child.

The glove-making interlude is also mentioned, and the article goes on to say that a branch of the Parisian Galitzines owned a department store, and the idea was that the young Yuri would learn the trade 'from the bottom'; with the intention of becoming the firm's English representative. Yuri hated the whole idea and particularly hated being sent to work as a labourer at a tannery in Millau, a glove-making centre in the Auvergne. There is no mention in the interview of his membership of the Right Club, or the robbery of his sister's valuables.

Another odd thing is that the piece says he was commissioned into his mother's old family regiment, the Royal Northumberland Fusiliers. Once again, this is the first mention of family involvement in such a regiment and one has to ask whether an element of fantasy was creeping into Yuri's recollections of his past. The official records for Yuri's, or Yurka's, military career do not mention this regiment.

Yuri's war experiences are described in some detail and then, in the summer of 1946, with demobilization 'there was the problem of what to do'. Apparently he joined the staff of the *Sunday Express* as a feature writer but soon realised that the hard graft of national newspaper journalism was not for him. He only lasted in the job for six months. After acting as Press Officer for a number of organisations, he decided to set up his own PR business in 1954. He had a working knowledge of six languages including Russian, and this was a great help in securing international commissions. His PR business became extremely successful, the interview concludes.

Prince Yuri is described as being fond of shooting and in fact, used to manage a shooting syndicate in Northamptonshire.

Since no mention is made of Pauline, one wonders where she was while the family was flitting about between Austria and France, or what Prince Nicholas himself was doing during this time. The quite long interview leaves tantalizing gaps on which, clearly, the interviewer did not prod her subject. We know that a naturalisation certificate was issued in 1928 for Pauline, although as yet no details were available. Did she travel with Nicholas and Elena to America, did she join them in Austria and France? Yuri never says a word about any of this.

The local Rutland people took Prince Yuri and Dr Jean Shanks to their hearts, much as the Waresley villagers had taken Prince Nicholas to their hearts. In both cases, they were proud to have a real Russian prince in their midst.

In 1994, Dr Shanks, under the name Princess Jean Galitzine, bought the run-down Holywell Hall near Stamford, Lincolnshire, for £4 million and set about enthusiastically renovating it. A local newspaper report says that the Hall was saved from dereliction by Princess Galitzine who had previously owned a house in the nearby village of Braunston. The house came with an 830-acre estate and was transformed into 'a modern Arcadia'.

Unfortunately Dr Shanks had only five years to live and she died on 11 November 1999 aged 74. In her Will she left £21 million, most of it to be used for the Jean Shanks Foundation. The pathology labs she founded continued to be in business until 2018.

Prince Yuri remained interested in Rutland's local history and on his own death in 2002 aged 83, left his large stack of papers and historical documents to the Rutland County Museum, where there is a Prince Yuri room. Rutland, the smallest county in England, remains extremely proud of its Prince Yuri connection and his obituary in the newsletter of the Rutland Local History Society has this to say:

> It may seem strange to some that a scion of a Russian aristocratic family should have taken such an interest in England's smallest county, but societies such as ours often owe much to people like Prince Yuri who find the time in their own busy lives to support and encourage them. He was proud of his Russian ancestry, and glad to have been able to visit that country in recent years. He was also proud of his association with his adoptive county, and we remember what he did for us and his support of the Society—and of the Rutland County Museum—with pride.

In his Will, Prince Yurka left around £7 million, so clearly the family fortunes, which had sunk so low as to see him apprenticed—apparently—in a glove-making factory had spectacularly revived. Once again, his Will is complicated but seems extremely fair in that he left equal shares to his four remaining children as well as many legacies to his employees, including a £30,000 bequest to Elizabeth Hannah Harvey, one of his executors. There are smaller bequests to his grandchildren and there is a great-grandchild, William.

In his book about Stanfield Hall, Dr Hudson writes that he is glad the house continued to be a private dwelling after he sold it in 1983 but Holywell Hall, so lovingly restored by Dr Jean Shanks, has become a wedding venue. Dr Hudson mourned the fact that so many grand houses were turned into nursing homes or hotels and yet, the money needed for their upkeep is way beyond the average pocket. Very often, the renovation costs far more than the actual purchase.

What are we to make of Prince Yurka? It seems as though he inherited a certain amount of flamboyance and theatricality from his father, and in 1964 it was reported in a magazine that he moved in 'elevated circles'. He was certainly a wow with the ladies, showing an actor-ish tendency to marry multiple times, and having at least one extra-marital affair. He also played heavily on his Russian ancestry and this gave him a certain exoticism he might not have had otherwise. Every single interview, newspaper report and write-up in books about the war mentions his noble Russian background.

As for his children, his son Gregory, an Oxford wine merchant, died aged 63 in 2018. According to Rory Knight Bruce, he walked with a limp and was known as Greg the Peg. Gregory was married to Svetlana, a consultant anaesthetist at the John Radcliffe Hospital, Oxford. Sophia never married and became a society interior designer.

Alexandra, the eldest daughter, seems to have disappeared from view and that leaves Catherine, the non-marital daughter who says she did not get to know her father until she was adult, as she was brought up by her mother as a single parent.

13

What became of Pauline's husbands?

THERE ARE ONLY scanty records for Pauline's first husband Reginald Ernest John Daubeny. After his divorce from Pauline, he married two more times. He had been born on 22 November 1909 at Glanford Bridge, Lincolnshire, and died at Rofield Barn, Lower Apperly in Gloucestershire, on 5 August 1995, aged 86, at Tewkesbury Hospital. His occupation was given on his death certificate as a retired business proprietor and the informant of his death was named as James Geoffrey Lennox Pugh.

Thinking that James Pugh might know something of Pauline, her first husband and Robin, I wrote to him and had the following reply:

Thank you for your letter.

I have no knowledge of Pauline (divorced before I was born!)

Reginald Ernest John Daubeny was always John as far as I am aware.

I knew Robin and that he had changed his name although I never asked the reason why.

Looks like I am unable to throw any further light upon your quest—sorry.

James Pugh

And that was as far as I could go. There is no record of Pauline and John Daubeny ever meeting again after the divorce and it seems she did all she could to avoid him when she learned that he was going to be a witness at Robin's first wedding.

More is known about Colin Dennistoun-Sword, the second husband. When he divorced Pauline in 1955 he was still only 40, but his health was fading. After Waresley he lived at Artillery Mansions for three years, then moving to Rest Harrow, near Lewes, his sister Eleanor's former house. She had married and gone to live in Canada and the house still belonged to her although it would revert to Colin should she die first. In the event Colin died on 28 February 1977, at 61, never having regained proper health after his POW injuries.

Rather like Prince Nicholas, there is no indication that Colin ever had another intimate relationship. When he died, he left £30,194 in his Will; equivalent to around £200,000 today. It was perhaps not a huge amount but reasonably respectable. Colin left £200 each to his sisters and to his partner in the genealogy firm, Joseph Deeny, and £25 each to a number of people including his former wife Pauline Sismey, for them all to enjoy a drink at his expense.

It seems from his Will that Colin had a financial interest in Westbourne Nursing Homes Ltd, as he bequeathed all of this to his co-director Elizabeth Anne Crichton Mortimer. No further details are given as to what his relationship, professional, business or personal, might have been to her. He also states in his Will that his family paintings, at present in the possession of his former wife Pauline Sismey, should be given to his cousin Henry Michael Dennistoun-Sword. There is no mention of Robin Winterbottom in Colin's Will and no indication that there was ever any kind of relationship between them, even though he would have been Colin's stepson (or possibly, actual son. That we might only know if either Johnathan or Paul Winterbottom, Robin's sons, might agree to do a DNA test. So far, they have not responded to requests.)

The indications from Colin's Will are that he remained fond of Pauline, for all that she divorced him, as indicated by the £25 he left her. Once again, though, there is no indication that they ever met after her marriage to Oliver Sismey.

Oliver, 11 years Pauline's senior, lived on at Offord Cluny Manor by himself until 1993 when he died aged 93. In his Will, dated 11 April 1991, he appointed his daughter Islay Anne Edwards as his executor along with Lady Judy Sophia Floyd, who had also been an executor of Pauline's Will in 1980. The third executor was Oliver's solicitor William Godfrey.

Lady Judy was the second wife of Sir Giles Floyd, born in 1932, who had been the High Sheriff of Rutland in 1968 and who was the chairman of the Burghley Estate Farms. There is a picture of Sir Giles, grinning broadly, with Princess Diana at the Burghley European Championships in 1989. Maybe the Rutland connection ties up with Prince Yurka's interest in the county, as Frances Sweeny, daughter of Margaret Duchess of Argyll, married Charles Manners, 10th Duke of Rutland, to become the Duchess of Rutland.

Somehow, everything ties up and I would imagine that Yurka himself, along with his fourth wife Jean Shanks, were also visitors at the Manor. And with her marriage to Oliver, Pauline was putting herself right at the centre of these grand families. Colin was a decent man from an upper-class background, but the truth was, he didn't have the connections in the area that Oliver Sismey had and if Pauline was finally going to make something of herself, she had to do it through an advantageous marriage.

I would guess that Pauline married twice for love and thirdly for position, and yet her third marriage was the one that lasted.

Among Oliver Sismey's bequests were £1000 to Mrs Joyce Jones; £1000 and his motor car to Keith Seelings, and £500 to Betty Swannell. All these were local people who had worked for Oliver during his last years. He also left £1000 towards the restoration of Offord Cluny church, where he had a family pew.

The main beneficiaries of his more than £500,000 estate were his daughter Islay and grandchildren Christopher and Annabel Edwards, with the money going to them in equal shares.

Among his wishes were a desire to be buried beside his late wife in Offord Cluny churchyard and for a joint tombstone to be erected over the grave of himself and his late wife, plus a memorial tablet to be erected near the Sismey family pew.

And so, with Oliver's death, and after more than 300 years, the Sismeys of Offord Cluny died out. The house, now in a near-derelict state, was sold and the only memories that remain are the joint tombstone, already practically unreadable, and the memorial tablet near the family pew. No member of the Sismey family has sat in the pew since Oliver died, and, it has to be said, very few people even now remember the Sismeys, for all that they were such a prominent family in the county for so many centuries.

Oliver's son-in-law Francis, the great would-be escapee, died in 2006 aged 88, meriting a major obituary in *The Times*. His daughter Islay lasted just 15 days after her husband and also died in 2006, aged 74. She had the famous mink coat to remember her stepmother by and one wonders whether, in turn, it was passed on to her daughter Annabel or whether by then, anti-fur activists had become so powerful that it could not be worn, sold or even given away.

Offord Cluny Manor, house and gardens, was restored by its next owner to its former glory and beyond, and all signs of the Sismeys' 300-year continuous occupation were obliterated. It now looks like a television show-home and its second sale, in 2016, made all the national newspapers. It was sold by the St Neots estate agents Fine and Country for £1.8 million. Estate agent Richard Carpenter said: 'It's a pleasure to be marketing this genuinely unique and historic home.' Much was made in the marketing pitch of Oliver Cromwell staying there during the English Civil War and that it had been in the ownership of the same family ever since it was first built in about 1600.

The current owners of Offord Cluny Manor, Charles and Jennifer Alexander, are directors of Cambridgeshire Lakes, a selection of holiday homes in Abbotsley, another nearby village. They have no connection of any kind with the Sismey family and are modern business people, not old-style gentry.

14

The mystery starts to unravel

ON A WALKING holiday with my ex-husband in November 2020, I discussed this story. I said to him, 'Pauline's father, who is named as Henry Stanley Turner on several certificates, doesn't seem to exist. And then, there is another mystery which is that Pauline originally had French nationality and this was confirmed by her third husband on her death certificate. And', I added, 'Pauline gave us a wedding present.'

My ex had no memory of her or the wedding present—I can't now remember what it was—but he immediately became excited. 'I think you should explore this,' he said. 'It seems clear to me that Pauline's father must have been somebody rich and important, and influential enough to be able to hide his identity for more than a century.'

This sent Neville off into wild speculations. 'I wonder whether he could have been George V, a youthful Charles de Gaulle or somebody like that. Whoever he was, he must have been the source of the money that enabled Princess Elena to live at such expensive addresses.'

George V? Charles de Gaulle? What a story if Pauline's father had been somebody as elevated as this. So when I was back at home I decided to try and get hold of the naturalisation certificate that I had discovered during a Google search. There were actually two naturalisation documents, both held at the National Archives, Kew. One, HO 334/120/195 was an 'open' certificate issued on 24 January 1928, and the other was a 'closed' certificate, identified as HO144/9707. Neither record had been digitised and the only way to view them was either to go in person or to order a copy. I decided to order a copy of the open certificate and to apply for permission to view the closed certificate in person, which I was told often contained more information than the open one as it would have the background to the naturalisation application.

A couple of weeks after I ordered the 'open' certificate it arrived in a special package—the post and packing cost £3.30 and I eagerly tore it open to see what it might reveal. It began by saying that under the British Nationality and Status of Aliens Act of 1914, the Certificate of Naturalization granted to a minor was issued on 24 January 1928 by Austen Chamberlain, the Foreign Secretary. He was the half-brother of future Prime Minister Neville Chamberlain and the certificate bears his signature.

The explanatory particulars are as follows:

Full Name: Pauline Vincent Turner
Address: 34 St John's Wood Court, Marylebone in the county of London.
Trade or occupation: Student.
Place and date of birth: Paris, France, 17 March 1912.
Nationality: French.
Names and nationality of parents: Henry Sutton Timmis, British, and Emma
Lilian Hodgson (known as Turner), British.

On the next page is the Oath of Allegiance, where 'Pauline Vincent Turner swore by Almighty God that she would be faithful and bear true allegiance to His Majesty, King George the Fifth, his Heirs and Successors, according to law'. There was also Pauline's signature in a round schoolgirl hand, very different from her later flourishing handwriting.

This revelation meant that the father was not somebody

particularly famous, but his name had cropped up before, as a witness at Pauline Turner's first wedding in 1931. Henry Sutton Timmis, Henry Stanley Turner; the initials were the same. And her real father was not deceased at the time but very much alive and very much present at her first wedding.

This means that I was right in guessing that there was no such person as Henry Stanley (or Suson) Turner. The name was clearly entered on the marriage certificates to put everybody off the scent but possibly, because the initials and the first name were the same, it was code for those in the know.

After receiving the certificate, a large two-page document, I looked up Henry Sutton Timmis and this is what I found:

Timmis, Henry Sutton. JP, Widnes. Eldest son of T.S. Timmis, born at Waterloo, July 8th, 1862; educated at Grove House, Tottenham Owens College, Manchester and Trinity College, Cambridge. BA Cantab. Partner in the firm of W. Gossage and Sons, Widnes, Director of Widnes and Runcorn Transporter Bridge, Justice of the Peace for the County of Lancaster; elected member of Widnes Local Board, 1888; elected Councillor and Alderman of the first Widnes Town Council, 1892. Chairman of the Gas and Water Committee since the formation of Council Member of the Committee of the Southern Hospital, and the Victoria District Nursing Association. Married, in 1890, Annie Hodgson Horsfall, fourth daughter of the late George Henry Horsfall, D.L, JP of Liverpool. Clubs: Palatine, Liverpool; Raleigh, London.

A solid and upright enough citizen, as it seems, busy busy and yet he found time to father a child out of wedlock. But as Toby Horton remarked when he saw the accompanying photograph, 'There is a twinkle in his eye!' As to how he tied up with the Winterbottoms, that was becoming closer as well. Timmis had been an executor for three Winterbottom wills by 1925 and an ancestor had been married to a Winterbottom. This made them cousins, even if quite distant by now. It also starts to explain Emma/Elena's close connection to the Winterbottoms, why she was such a frequent guest at their various functions and also, why her daughter Pauline had her son adopted by them. As the Winterbottom and Timmis families were so close, it is very likely, in fact more than likely, that George and Penelope were in on the secret of Pauline's paternity. If so, they never let on, publicly at least. It may also have been that George and Penelope felt slightly sorry for Pauline carrying the stigma of illegitimacy and that had also been a factor in the adoption.

Henry Timmis's civic upright reputation could have been ruined if it was widely known that he had fathered an illegitimate daughter with a woman 26 years his junior, even though such liaisons were not all that uncommon.

Susan Dorey, who had mentioned Timmis in her Winterbottom book, said: 'It is my theory that Pauline was conceived in England—which must have been June or July 1911. In 1911 her mother Emma and grandmother lived across the Mersey from Liverpool, while Henry Timmis lived in Liverpool. Once she was pregnant, Henry sent her to France.'

Henry Sutton Timmis's father had been a partner in the Gossage soap business and had died a rich man. Henry himself had three legitimate children: Joan, Eileen and Richard. Richard was educated at Eton and Sandhurst Royal Military Academy and was killed in the First World War, aged 19. Joan died just five days after birth and Eileen, the only child to outlive him, never married. This meant that the Timmis family died out on Henry's death in 1942, although in a way it continues with Robin Winterbottom's family.

If Henry Sutton Timmis was not exactly famous, he was certainly rich. Very rich. He left over £50 million in today's money when he died in 1942.

It is not too far a stretch now, to see how Henry Timmis became Pauline's father. Emma Hodgson had trained as a stenographer. The likelihood is that she went to work in the soap factory and caught the eye of her boss, two decades her senior and married with two surviving children. They had an affair, the usual thing happened, the 23-year-old became pregnant and panic stations ensued. Timmis could not risk a scandal. Susan Dorey wondered whether Timmis's wife Annie Hodgson, had some connection to the Fawcett-Hodgson family, but could not find anything.

This revelation tells us something about Emma, though, as not only did she attract her boss enough to become pregnant by him, but she had also inveigled a young Russian prince, nine years her junior.

My ex-husband also reckoned that Pauline must have had some charms herself to have attracted three husbands in quick succession. That is most probably true, but her mother had, too. As of course did Prince Yurka. Prince Nicholas himself was a Prince Charming, by all accounts, so the whole family was loaded down with charm and charisma. None of them were people you could exactly ignore.

But I needed to get at the rest of the story as there were no particular details in the 'open' certificate as to how Pauline came to be born in France or how she acquired French nationality when both of her parents were British. I had to see whether I could obtain permission to view the closed document. It was worth a try.

I contacted the National Archives and a few weeks later had the following response:

Dear Miss Hodgkinson

Thank you for your enquiry regarding a review of:

HO144/9797—Nationality and Naturalization: Turner, Pauline Vincent, from France. Resident in London. Certificate C.195 issued 24 January 1928.

We are pleased to tell you that it has been decided that this record can now be made available to the public at The National Archives, Kew.

The record will be opened, a process that usually takes up to 5 working days.

However, as we are still experiencing some disruption (post-lockdown) it may take slightly longer. Please check our online catalogue, Discovery, for the latest status of the record.

We have handled your request under the Freedom of Information Act 2000.

The FOI Act gives you the right to know whether we hold the information you want and to have it communicated to you.

Then follows the somewhat complicated procedure to gain access to the records but the upshot was that I had been granted permission under the Freedom of Information Act 2000 to view the document, nine years earlier than it was officially declared open. That sounded like a breakthrough, indeed. I applied for a Reader's Ticket—no easy matter even though there was no charge, and it took me several attempts—and I arranged to go to Kew to view the documents in person. I was informed that I was not allowed to take anything into the Reading Room such as a handbag, pen or paper, but I was permitted to photocopy the records.

I had to tell them in advance which day I would be arriving and about what time as although the Reading Room was now open, it was operating on reduced hours and was, in the phrase that had become all too common in 2020, 'Covid secure'. Once I finally received my reader's ticket, I then had to look at the available time slots and was astonished to discover that the Reading Room was full for about a week. Eventually I found a space and quickly booked it. Then I had to plan my journey from Oxford to Kew.

Having lived in Richmond for many years I knew the area well and remembered that the National Archives building was only a few minutes' walk from the station.

On Friday 11 December 2020, I made my epic journey to the Archives, arriving at about 11 o'clock. I then had to go through the very tough Security procedures and wondered at every step whether I really had got permission, whether the documents actually existed and whether all my papers were in order. I had previously had to download my reader's ticket and bring it with me. It was a very precious document indeed as without it I would not have been allowed inside the building. Once inside, everything had to match: the date, the time, the purpose of my visit—had I got the document details correct?—and then they took a photo. They were not taking any chances. After about half an hour I was informed that everything was present and correct, so that was another hurdle over.

The next job was to go to the cloakroom to divest myself of my coat, handbag and all personal possessions except for my phone and i-Pad, which I was allowed to take into the Reading Room with me. I had decided to take both devices in case one didn't work, the battery went flat or some other electronic disaster meant that I couldn't photograph the records.

I had been allocated a specific locker in which to store my things and that took a bit of finding among the many rows of lockers. I then had to go back to the Registration area and be allotted a seat in the Reading Room. 'The documents are ready and waiting for you,' said the chap at the desk. 'They are in your own locker upstairs. You can photocopy the documents and take the photocopies home with you, or if you prefer, you can order a copy to be sent to you.'

Having come this far, I didn't want to risk the possibility that not everything would be copied, or that an important element would not be missed out, so I said I would do all the photocopying myself. There is never anything to beat going through documents yourself and even though I was not allowed to take notes, making photocopies would probably be better as I would then get a permanent record of the actual records, which I could then print out at home.

Finally, once I had got the folder in my hands, I had to take it to the Reading Room where there was yet more security and find my seat. I was told that the Room was full but in fact it was three-quarters empty as social distancing rules at the time meant that 'full' had been redefined as 'nearly empty'. But at last I could sit down and go through all the papers. It was exciting and scary in equal amounts and I had to be prepared for an astonishing revelation, or nothing very much. I was relieved to find that the folder was quite thick, which must mean there was something there.

It was just as well that I went when I did as two weeks later the Archives building was closed again 'until further notice'. I had just managed to squeeze in between lockdowns.

But was it to be journey's end?

15

All is revealed!

THE APPLICATION FOR naturalisation is not a simple matter. It is dry and official in tone but there are, here and there, attempts to humanise it. I think the best thing is to reproduce it exactly as it was written in 1928.

The application is headed: METROPOLITAN POLICE, SPECIAL BRANCH, SCOTLAND HOUSE, and is dated 11 January 1928.

Although the following was the first document in the folder, it was composed after much research into the genuineness of the application, and after taking statements from 'respectable' people who knew Pauline and the family well.

It reads:

With reference to the application for a certificate of naturalization by Pauline VINCENT, generally known as Pauline Vincent TURNER of 34 St John's Wood, NW8:

I beg to report that the applicant's correct name is Pauline VINCENT. She is the holder of a birth certificate dated 30 August 1927, issued by the Mairie, Paris, which shows that she was born on 17 March 1912, at 40, Rue La Perouse, Paris, and which has been produced. The certificate is in the name of Pauline Vincent: it does not state the nationality of the parents and neither the father's nor the mother's name is given.

Enquiry shows that the applicant was born out of wedlock, her mother being

166

(Miss) Emma Lilian HODGSON, then known as Mrs Turner and her acknowledged father Henry Sutton TIMMIS, both British subjects. Applicant remained in the care of her mother, and about seven weeks after her birth was brought to this country for her up-bringing. As her mother was still using the name of Mrs Turner, the girl was known as Pauline Vincent Turner, and it is by that name that she has been known at school and generally among friends. In 1918 her mother was married to Prince Nicholas Galitzine, a Little Russian, and since that time the applicant has also been known at school at Pauline Turner or Golitzin, but for all general purposes her name has been given as Pauline Turner.

When she is not at school applicant's permanent address is 34, St John's Wood Court, NW8 where she resides with her maternal grandmother, Mrs Margaret Hodgson, a British subject. This address is closely situated to that of her mother, Princess Galitzine, at 28 Elm Tree Road, NW8 and the girl spends her time fairly equally between the two places, although her settled home is with her grandmother and the latter has been appointed her legal guardian.

Applicant is a French subject but, apart from the birth certificate mentioned above, she has no French documents. On the few occasions when she has been out of this country she has been shown on her grandmother's British passport. In October 1919 applicant became a pupil at the girls' school, Heathfield, Ascot, and she has continued there until the present time. It is now desired that she be sent during the coming spring to commence a year's course at a school in Italy, to be followed later by a similar period in France, to complete her education, following which she intends to return to this country and reside permanently herein.

The total length of her residence within the United Kingdom is, with the exception of the first seven weeks of her life and occasional short holiday visits to the Continent with her grandmother, the whole of her life. She is continuing temporarily at Heathfield School, where she has been for the past eight years, and she has an adequate knowledge of the English language. She has acknowledged her signature to the memorial as genuine.

The declaration of the memorialist's residence has been enquired into and found correct, the residence shown having been her permanent home, either with her mother or grandmother, during the periods when she was not at school.

According to enquiry, memorialist [the term given to the applicant] is a respectable girl. Metropolitan Police records have been searched but nothing to her detriment is known by police. Her mother, Princess Galitzine, is duly registered at Bow Street as a Russian subject under serial no. C22441 and is the holder of registration certificate no. 337863; Prince Nicholas Galitzine is also registered under serial C22411, and holds registration certificate no.110665, and nothing to the detriment of either is known by police.

The applicant appears to be a quiet, retiring girl. She is being well educated and is a highly intelligent person. She thoroughly understands the meaning and importance of the oath of allegiance and states that she has always regarded herself as British in every way, and desires to be in fact, as she is in sentiment, a true British subject.

Applicant has recently been made fully aware of the true facts of her birth. For many years, she has known her father as 'Uncle' and the latter regards himself as responsible for her welfare. He frequently meets her in the company of her mother, and a very warm affection exists between them. Mr Timmis, who resides at 4 Croxteth Road, Liverpool, has made various financial settlements upon applicant, which now amounts to approximately £21,000; the money is invested chiefly in Government stock in this country and is administered by the British Public Trustee. Applicant's financial position can therefore be said to be quite satisfactory. The actual amount of the settlement has been kept secret from Princess Galitzine and applicant's interests are in the hands of her grandmother, Mrs Hodgson who, as already stated, is her responsible legal guardian.

Particulars of applicant's birth certificate and of her use of various names have not been shown in answer to nos 5 and 6 of the questionnaire, but, with this exception, the questionnaire has been correctly answered.

The referees are respectable, responsible persons, householders and natural-born British subjects. They both speak of memorialist as a respectable girl and both vouch for her loyalty to this country.

Residence referee Arthur Cadogan BLUNT of 194 Cheyne Walk, sw, an artist of independent means, has known memorialist practically the whole of her life. He is a close personal friend of the family and of the applicant's father and is intimately acquainted with the whole of applicant's affairs and private life. He has had personal knowledge of applicant's residence at each of the addresses shown, gained through the regular interchange of social visits; he speaks of her in high terms as a very steady and modest young girl and considered her in every way deserving of British naturalization. He has acknowledged his signature as genuine.

Referee the Rev. Thomas Henry PASSMORE, of 3E Hyde Park Mansions, W2 and St John the Baptist's church, Great Marlborough Street, W. has not been interviewed. He is at present out of the Metropolitan Police District, temporarily residing at the Fleur de Lis Hotel, Canterbury, Kent, and is not expected to return home until at least the 21st instant. Mrs Passmore, however, has been seen, and has acknowledged the declaration as that of her husband. She is acquainted, equally, with her husband concerning the memorialist, and states that they have known the latter practically the whole of her life, through the fact that they are close personal friends of her mother and family generally. They move in the same circles and exchange social visits with Princess Galitzine and have a good knowledge of the memorialist's private life and general character. Mrs Passmore speaks of applicant as a very refined and steady girl and considered her a very fit and proper person for the grant of British naturalization.

The document is signed by Ralph Mitchener or Kitchener (signature unclear) who describes himself as a Sergeant.

As can be deduced by this document, much red tape had already been completed before the document was presented to the Home Secretary, and Pauline herself had to fill in a detailed questionnaire which she did, in very neat handwriting. In the space for parents, she writes: 'My father Henry Sutton Timmis, 4 Croxteth Road, Liverpool, my mother, now Princess Galitzine, 28 Elm Tree Road, NW8'.

As part of the application, Princess Elena had to write to the Home Secretary, Sir William Joynson-Hicks, in support of her daughter's application, and her letter sheds an interesting light on her character and attitude.

She writes, on 30 December 1927, from her home address of 28 Elm Tree Road, in educated handwriting, on blue headed unlined notepaper:

Dear Sir William

I am enclosing the necessary papers already signed referring to my daughter Pauline's petition for naturalization, together with my cheque for £1.

Knowing that it is necessary for you to institute the fullest enquiries I am enclosing a letter from the Principal of Heathfield (School) Ascot where she has been at school since she was seven years old—to prove the fact and I pray to obviate the necessary (sic) of sending someone down to the school to avoid scandal for the child's sake as she will always wish to continue going there to old girls' gatherings and could never do so if these facts were known as the Head Mistress is a great snob and extremely narrow minded!

She spells Galitzine as Galitzine because when my husband first came to England attached to the Russian mission, he translated the Russian (Galitzine appears here in Russian characters) literally but as the Russian o is pronounced a and also other members of the family came to London who preferred to use the French form of spelling. We have for some years used that form and find it is much more convenient.

I am troubling you with all this as I have a great wish to make everything absolutely clear in every way—and trust that I have done so.

May I take this opportunity of thanking you for the great courtesy and consideration that I have received in to me such a difficult situation—and I trust that some time I shall have the opportunity of thanking you personally.

As my husband and I are going to stay with friends at (Russian place name) for three weeks leaving town 25 January would it be possible for the necessary enquiries to be made before then?

I should be so grateful if this could be so as I can make no plans for my daughter to go to school in Italy for a year—as she wishes at Easter—until this matter is settled and I am naturally very anxious.

With all good wishes for the New Year and again many thanks for your kindness.

I remain

Yours sincerely

E. Lilian Galitzine.

We can see that here is a highly intelligent, sensitive and also persuasive woman who wants the best for her daughter and who, at the same time, sees herself on quite a level with the Home Secretary. The tone of her letter is intimate and confiding, while at the same time having the necessary formality for such an important process. It is a masterpiece of a letter, I would say. Who could refuse such a plea?

Along with her letter, Princess Elena enclosed a note from that 'great snob and narrow minded' headmistress (and founder) of Heathfield School, Miss Wyatt.

This note, once again in handwriting, on writing paper headed HEATHFIELD, ASCOT, and dated 29 December 1927, reads:

> I have pleasure in stating that Miss Pauline V Turner, known to us as Pauline Golitzin, daughter of Princess Nicolas Galitzine, has been a pupil at Heathfield since October 1919 when she entered the school at the age of 7 years.

The letter is signed with a flourish by E. Beatrice Wyatt.

In view of the many references to Heathfield School in the naturalisation documents, it is extremely odd that the school's archivist, Karen Hunt, could not find a single reference to Pauline's having attended the establishment, especially when she had been there for nine years.

As it happened, the application was quickly processed, thanks in large part to Princess Elena's heartfelt and very honest letter explaining the delicate situation and the naturalisation was granted by 25 January 1928, when Princess Elena wrote again to Sir William Joynson-Hicks: once again on headed paper from 28 Elm Tree Road and with the telephone number Paddington 5565, the short letter reads:

> Dear Sir William
> I am enclosing my daughter Pauline's certificate of naturalization for registration and do thank you *so* sincerely for granting this so speedily.
> It has taken a load off my mind.
>
> Yours sincerely
> E. Lilian Galitzine.

From all the above, it may seem as though the naturalisation proceeded without a hitch, but this was not quite the case. Although the Metropolitan Police document makes a seemingly watertight case for naturalisation, the many name changes worried some of the officials examining the application.

On the first page of the document, some jobs-worth writes: 'I do not see why we should swallow "Pauline Vincent". The mother's name will appear on the cert as Hodgson, so I think that the memorial should show the girl's name as Pauline Hodgson, known as Pauline Vincent Turner (described on her birth cert as Pauline Vincent)'.

A response, in different handwriting, objects to this, saying: 'As far as I can see the girl has never been known as Hodgson and the name Vincent seems to have been invented for the French birth certificate. She is called Turner, (or Golitzine) and she may be called Pauline Vincent Turner on the certificate.'

At any rate, Prince and Princess Galitzine could now go off safely to see their friends in Russia in the knowledge that the process was complete and that for all purposes in future, Pauline was now a British subject.

The document also gives the various addresses where Pauline, her mother or her grandmother had lived since 1915, as required by the Home Office. They are:

From 1915 to 1919: 17 Grove End Road, London NW8
From 1919 to 1921: 28 Elm Tree Road, London NW8
From 1921 to 1923: 39 Gloucester Terrace, London W2
From 1923 to 1927: 34 St John's Wood Court, London NW8

The requirement for these addresses was to prove that Pauline had, in fact, spent most of her life in London and not in Paris. All, it will be seen, are upmarket London addresses and the wherewithal to buy or rent them must have been provided by Henry Sutton Timmis, as neither Emma Hodgson nor her mother had any money to speak of. Obviously, Timmis could not marry Emma but he certainly did the next best thing by her and looked after the family handsomely. Of course, he had the money to do so, but he also went to great lengths to keep his extra-marital daughter's existence secret and to remain secret. This secrecy clearly could not continue when the application for naturalisation came up. I imagine that Pauline, who wanted to study abroad, would not have been able to do so unless she had a British passport of her own and for this to be achieved, the secret finally had to come out. Otherwise, her paternity might have remained hidden all her life and she might never have known who her true father was.

The absence of a birth certificate, though, might have caused problems when Pauline wanted to get married, aged 19. As it was, the certificate (untraceable) was only issued in 1927 with no parents being named. That might have seemed strange, as well, and one wonders whether Pauline told her three husbands of the peculiar circumstances of her birth.

It seems from the foregoing that Pauline had expressed a wish to learn Italian and for this, wanted to go to Italy for a year, and it put her mother in a difficult situation. If naturalisation was to be granted, the full story of how and why a British person somehow had French nationality had to come out and yet, in a way, it didn't. The naturalisation documents do not say anywhere how it was that Pauline, then a baby, became a French citizen when neither of her parents was French, she was only in the country for seven weeks anyway, and no birth certificate was issued until 1927, when she was 15. No wonder nobody was able to find such a certificate as it didn't exist in the first place, and it would not have occurred to any of us to start looking for a birth certificate for somebody aged 15. Once again, one assumes that Timmis, who was a Director of the Liverpool Overhead Railway in addition to his many other business interests, had connections in high places and was able to pull strings. He must have known somebody in Paris who would look after the mother and baby during the birth and immediately after, as there are no indications that Emma had any French connections. All that must have cost money too, so all in all it was an expensive process keeping Pauline's paternity concealed.

Did she ever wonder where all the money came from, not only for her mother and stepfather to live in an expensive house, but also her grandmother, and to send her to Heathfield as a boarder from the age of seven? And then, the naturalisation document refers to holidays spent on the Continent; once again, very few people in those days had holidays abroad. The sugar daddy continued to provide, certainly until Pauline was adult and most probably paid for the year in Italy as well. Pauline must have realised that the only real way to learn a language was to go to the country and immerse yourself in it. That way, you will eventually be able to speak the language in a way that can never happen when you are taught in the schoolroom.

In her memoir, *Wait for Me!* Deborah, Duchess of Devonshire and the youngest Mitford sister, writes that she never learned to speak French because, unlike her sisters, she had never been sent to France for a year as a teenager. Pauline Turner's year in Italy, and subsequent year in France, must have been why she was called 'a clever linguist' in the 1939 newspaper report of her second marriage to Colin Dennistoun-Sword. It was quite common in the 1920s and 30s for the aristocracy to send teenage children to France or Italy for a year to enable them to speak the languages, and Pauline was at least an honorary member of the upper classes.

There are many novels about squires and other dastardly seducers getting lowly servants pregnant and then deserting them—Barbara Taylor Bradford's blockbuster *A Woman of Substance* hangs on such a plot—but the heartening true tale of Emma and her daughter Pauline suggests that not all young women met this tragic fate. Indeed, it is hard to see how, under the circumstances, they could have done any better.

There is a similar skeleton in the cupboard in the Winterbottom family. William Dickson Winterbottom, the older brother of George Harold Winterbottom 1, had a long affair with a housemaid, Rosa, who became pregnant and had a child called Ivy. This was actually Rosa's second pregnancy, but William Dickson was not the father of the first child. Once again, it seems clear from the records that William Dickson looked after Rosa and did not turn her out in the streets.

As it was, the illegitimate birth of Pauline, and the money showered on Emma as a result, enabled her to take her place in the upper reaches of London society. By 1928 she had left her relatively modest Liverpool upbringing far behind and was now, as well as living in some splendour with live-in servants of her own, a Russian Princess, a somebody.

Although her letters to Sir William Joynson-Hicks do not press the point, it is clear from their confident yet confiding tone that she considered herself quite on a level with the Home Secretary. She was, by this time, mixing in similar social circles as the naturalisation application suggests. The Rev. T.H. Passmore had been a witness at Emma's marriage to Prince Nicholas, so had been a family friend for many years. Arthur Cadogan Blunt was an artist, illustrator, etcher and poster designer whose highly decorative works were popular at the turn of the last century. The Mary Vue Blunt who was also a witness at Emma's wedding must have been Mrs Blunt, the artist's wife. It was true, then that these people had known the family for many years.

In the matter of Pauline being presented at court in 1930, once again it is more than likely that Henry Timmis footed the bill for the dresses, the dances and all the other necessities of the Season.

As to the birth in Paris, this was no doubt arranged so that not the tiniest whiff of scandal could touch the respective families. Paris was far enough away in those days. Henry Timmis had interests in shipping companies and it would have been relatively easy for him to arrange for Emma to board a ship from Liverpool to France and from there to make her way to Paris where arrangements were made for her to be looked after during the pregnancy and birth. And then, it would be politic to return to London rather than to Liverpool, where awkward questions might be asked. It was also a clever move to spirit Pauline's grandmother to London, as if Margaret Hodgson was not in Liverpool, she could not be quizzed about what had happened to her daughter. Having her around also meant that Princess Elena was relieved of childcare duties, so these were neat solutions all round, facilitated by large sums of money.

By living now in London, a husband, Mr Turner, could be invented and then conveniently disappear or die. It was all very well planned and one imagines that Timmis's wife and children had no idea that this was happening. They might never have known and in the days when rich husbands routinely concealed their true wealth from their wives, need not either have known about the large sums of money regularly leaking out to support another family.

And then, six years after Pauline's birth, and with her 'husband' dead—a story could have been invented whereby he was killed during the First World War—Emma achieved respectability and then some by marrying a Russian prince and becoming a princess. The fact that she was described as a 'spinster' on her marriage certificate to Prince Nicholas was confusing for a while, but although there was no evidence until the naturalisation papers came to light, it became obvious that Pauline must have been illegitimate and that there was a very good reason for hiding her father's identity.

Even after the paternity could be hidden no longer, I imagine it was still kept secret from as many people as possible. After all, the naturalisation documents were closed during the lifetime of all the important participants in the story. 'Not a whisper of this story comes out in the huge book about the Galitzines that my father had commissioned,' said Catherine Horwood-Barwise. 'This suggests to me that he never knew about it.' Heathfield School probably never knew about it either; as Princess Elena explains in her letter to Sir William Joynson-Hicks, her greatest fear is that the scandal might come out.

The school's current website says that the establishment educates girls from the age of 11 to 18 and does not mention admitting pupils younger than this. Seven years old is very young to be a boarder but we do have Miss Wyatt's letter confirming Pauline Golitsyn as a pupil from this age, so in the past the school must have admitted younger girls.

One might imagine that Timmis paid dear for his indiscretion with his secretary, as at the same time as sending his secret daughter to Heathfield and setting her mother up in expensive houses, even after her marriage to Prince Nicholas, he settled a very large sum on Pauline. £21,000 in 1938 amounts to around £1.3 million today. £21,000 would not be a bad sum for a 16-year-old to have today; it would go a long way towards paying off student debt, for instance, and it certainly meant that Pauline was a rich young lady. In 1928 such a sum was an absolute fortune; no wonder young men flocked around and that at the age of 19, as an heiress, more or less, she married the 21-year-old Reginald Daubeny.

One cannot help wondering whether she knew, or suspected, as a child, that her 'Uncle' was actually her father, or guessed at least. Maybe by the age of 16, she was too old to be particularly traumatised by the revelation, yet if she was as intelligent a child as her referees stated, she would certainly have had some inclination that this 'Uncle', who unaccountably showered so much largesse on her, was no ordinary uncle. She may also have wondered why she was never allowed to meet his family, his wife and daughter; his other two children having died by then.

Since Pauline was informed of her paternity certainly by the age of 16 and it is also recorded on the official naturalisation certificate of 1928, one wonders why the pretence was kept up, not just at her first wedding, but also at her second and third weddings as well, that Henry Stanley Turner, deceased, was her father. Henry Timmis was even a witness at her first wedding. By now, surely, everybody would know the truth? And yet, Princess Elena may have wished to maintain the pretence because of Heathfield, as the school magazine records that Pauline did in fact attend old girls' gatherings after her first marriage.

So now we know that the money that Timmis settled on his daughter comprised the mysterious Princess Pauline Galitzine Settlement, lodged with the Public Trustee and to which I was not allowed access. There may not have been much left, however, by the time Pauline died in 1980.

And what about Emma's marriage to the young Prince? Catherine Horwood-Barwise said that he had fallen head over heels in love with her and also, that he had no money of his own. This did not need to worry Emma as she had plenty of money which continued to be provided by Timmis. Timmis also prudently ensured that neither she nor Prince Nicholas could raid Pauline's settlement as the naturalisation proposal states that it was kept hidden. This means that although extremely generous, he remained firmly in control, as a typical Victorian entrepreneur. Everything had to be on his terms.

What he thought when his cover was necessarily blown, is not recorded. But once the naturalisation certificate was issued, it could have been shown to anybody, including Timmis's business and civic associates. But it seems that scandal was avoided, even after the truth came out. There was, perhaps, the opportunity for blackmail, but everybody concerned remained honourable.

Certainly, whilst there were rumours that Pauline had a secret son, even before she mentioned him to my mother, nobody ever gossiped about her being illegitimate. There were of course illegitimate children in St Neots, as everywhere else, but nobody ever whispered: 'Mrs Sismey gives herself such airs but she was born out of wedlock, you know.'

When Henry Timmis died in 1942, he left over £1 million, amounting to about £50 million today. His Will was very simple and straightforward. There is no mention of his other family, and his wealth was to be divided equally between his wife Annie and spinster daughter Eileen. This was after generous bequests of £8000 were made to Liverpool College and £5000 to the Liverpool United Hospital.

It may well have been that when Timmis died, the source of the money stopped and this was one reason why Prince and Princess Nicholas Galitzine came to live at The Red House in Waresley full-time and in relatively reduced circumstances, although Princess Elena retained some private income, as revealed in her Will, where she left around £7000; the equivalent of £300,000 today. Pauline's grandmother also went to live at The Red House and the London homes were given up.

It is interesting to note that, in spite of all the subterfuge that went into hiding Pauline's illegitimacy, if, instead of being taken to

Paris, Emma Hodgson had given birth in London, the true paternity might never have come out, as there would never have been any need for it to be revealed for the naturalisation process. I imagine that both Princess Elena and Henry Timmis had kittens when Pauline announced that she wished to study abroad, as the truth could then no longer be concealed. A British passport could not have been issued to a French national, as Pauline still was at that point. Nor would she had been able to have a French passport. But for this, the fiction of Henry Stanley Turner being her father could have been maintained for ever.

One mystery that will probably never be solved is why Emma Hodgson called herself 'Turner' and why she used the name Turner on her marriage certificate when she had never legally possessed any such name. Was it because it was the closest she felt she could get to Timmis without anybody cottoning on? The name certainly threw the naturalisation officials into some confusion. And 'Pauline Vincent Turner' did not officially exist until she was 15 years old, as her birth was not registered either in France or in England. This was probably why she had been known as Pauline Golitsyn at Heathfield. At least Prince Nicholas Golitsyn (spellings vary on all documents) was her recognised stepfather, even if he never legally adopted her as such.

Susan Dorey wondered whether the names 'Vincent' and 'Turner' were used because Emma/Elena was keen on art. That is a possibility, especially as the artist Arthur Cadogan Blunt was a close friend and Elm Tree Road was a particularly arty enclave, but it remains an unverifiable speculation.

How far might those early lies, no doubt entered into with the best protective intention, have affected Pauline's personality? When I first met her, she had a remote air about her as if to say: don't get too close. Even the scent she wore seemed to say, keep your distance, and people did feel slightly nervous around her. And although she dropped hints to my mother about a noble Russian heritage and of being born in Paris, nobody ever knew the full story. It was as if concealment had become an embedded part of her nature. She threw out tiny nuggets which somehow precluded further questioning and kept herself mysterious right to the end. Even her closest friends and neighbours never knew much about her, as evidenced by the Duberlys and the Edmunds not even knowing she had a son. She was just this slightly scary lady in a mink coat, rumoured to have numerous affairs, something of an adventuress, alighting in this little corner of East Anglia from nobody knew where, and attracting husbands from top public schools.

I always had an inkling that she had much to hide and she certainly took her secrets to the grave and beyond. I would say that she was the only mysterious person in the whole of Huntingdonshire, at least during my time there, like somebody out of a novel; the stranger who descends from nobody knows where and creates havoc in a local community. Everybody else I knew, or knew about, during my childhood, was an open book and there was not the slightest mystery about them. Perhaps that was why she intrigued me so much, as most people in St Neots and District were dull and boring, not to put too fine a point on it. Even the other great ladies who came into my mother's shop were not all that interesting, coming from solid local farming stock and marrying into each other's families.

16
The end of the flower shop

AS MY MOTHER got older and frailer and less able to resist, Richard became ever more bullying and controlling. Mum made him a director of the business and he forced her to retire. But it was worse; he gained access to all her money. As so often with people who are not particularly bright, he was able to exert a combination of low cunning, cajoling and coercion.

One day my ex-husband visited her as he did from time to time. While he was there, Mum said to him: 'Richard's got all my money.'

'What do you mean?' he asked.

'Oh yes, a solicitor's been round and I've signed the forms.' She was starting to become slightly confused by now and I don't think she really understood what it was all about. It was probably all done in the guise of helping a poor old lady, which is how the solicitor would have presented it, I'm sure.

When Neville and I were next in touch, he told me what had happened. 'That must mean he has got lasting power of attorney,' I said. Neville also reported to me the state of the house. Richard's second marriage had ended and he was back living in the Avenue Road house. Neville said there were pizza boxes all over the floor and the grass in the garden was at least a foot high. The whole place had an air of deep neglect and although Richard had not been there when Neville called round, it was clear that he had his own key and came and went as he liked. I wondered: should I go and see for myself, and if so, what could I do?

First, I called her on the phone. 'Neville says that Richard has got all your money,' I said. 'Is it true?'

'Yes,' she said, quite cheerfully as if it was the best news in the world. 'The solicitor has been round.'

'So Neville said. What's this all about? Why wasn't I consulted about this?'

'I want Richard to do everything,' she said. 'So you can just stop interfering.' I decided then not to go and visit her in person. There was no point and I didn't want to confront Richard, who by now had all the power; the power of the powerless.

Of course, lasting power of attorney means that to all intents and purposes, the person in whom the power is vested, is effectively not you. They can sign all cheques, take as much money out of your bank account as they like and you cannot prevent them as you have signed away your rights. Signing over lasting power of attorney to Richard meant that he was now in control of everything. A worse person to whom to hand over one's financial affairs could be hardly be imagined.

'I thought,' I said, 'that you told me you were going to leave the house to me and the shop and business to Richard. That was what you said.'

'But the shop's losing so much money,' she said. 'It's in deep debt.'

'That's not my fault,' I told her. But she had long stopped being able to listen to reason. Apart from anything else, early dementia had set in.

I sensed that Richard was in the background, listening. 'I don't want you to interfere,' she said. 'I want Richard to handle everything. You just go away. I want Richard to do everything.' She had completely changed allegiance and Richard had poisoned her against me so much that she no longer wanted to see me. 'You only come about three times a year,' she said, 'and Richard is here all the time.'

She also let slip that Richard had forbidden her friends and neighbours to call round, thus isolating her in the kind of elder abuse that has become quite common with elderly parents who are beginning to suffer from dementia, and the adult children who prey on them. But so often, these elderly parents become pathetically dependent on their abusers.

When the Pindreds, who had run the grocery business next door, retired, Richard acquired that shop as well and expanded the business to what had been two separate shops. The Pindreds continued to live in the flat above and Richard became effectively their landlord. It didn't take him long to run the whole enterprise into the ground. Thelma had long left as she could not stand working with Richard, thinking him lazy and stupid, and Mum's other assistants had fled as well. Even before Richard forced her to retire and took over the business completely, staff kept leaving. Mum said to me once, 'They don't like working with Richard,' but still championed him over all sense and reason.

Eventually, Mum had to go into a care home. I did not even know which one as Richard and I had long stopped speaking and he refused to give me any information about her. Then one day he called to say that she had died. 'I don't suppose you're going to the funeral, are you?' he asked.

'Probably not,' I said. She was cremated at Bedford Crematorium. Richard had sold the Avenue Road house for about £235,000, as I learned from looking up the sale on the Land Registry. And, amazingly, he had married again and gone to live with his new wife in St Ives. Local millionaire Ivan Twigden said to me once that all his wives must have had a death wish: 'It's the only thing that explains it.' Ivan himself had also been married three times so maybe he was not an absolute authority on marital longevity.

I discovered that when she died, Mum had less than £5000 in her estate; a figure too low for probate to be applied. I got nothing, nothing whatever from her life, never mind no money. It didn't really matter because I had absented myself from St Neots for decades and once Richard got control of the shop—anybody less competent to run a business could hardly be imagined—it was difficult to see Mum on her own. He was always hanging around, always liable to barge into her house and start shouting the odds and listening to what was being said.

So what happened to Richard after our mother died? He did everybody a favour and died too, maybe six months later. I was working up in my office one evening when I saw an email from my niece, Richard's daughter Samantha. It said that Richard had been taken into hospital for some apparently minor procedure and had died suddenly, aged about 60. The shop had been deep in debt and there were no assets.

Suddenly I felt that the fog had lifted, that I could visit St Neots again without the lowering and hostile presence of Richard who, I have to say, I had not allowed to blight my life. But he had always been hanging around in the background and one never knew when he might pounce. At least he never asked me for money. I think that even he realised there would be no point, however much he might use emotional blackmail and wheedling on other people.

By now, there was nobody left of my early life. Parents, brother, mother's customers, had all gone. St Neots itself, too, had changed out of all recognition, not just geographically but socially as well.

I suppose that I was one of the lucky ones because not only did I escape St Neots by going to university, I managed to carve out a life for myself that had nothing to do with my lowly origins. Although it may sound callous, sometimes the only strategy for survival is to cut off one's family of origin and have nothing more to do with them. You may keep hoping they will change and turn into decent people but sadly, that will never happen. Although not a 'bolter'—not in the marital sense at least—I certainly bolted from my home town at the earliest opportunity and never went back.

After university, aged 21, I married Neville Hodgkinson, a tall, elegant and ambitious young man who, on graduation, became a trainee reporter on the local paper, the Evening Chronicle. I first got a job as a teacher in local secondary schools in the North-East and then started writing for local papers. Our sons Tom and Will were both born in Newcastle and so are technically Geordies. We had a good time in Newcastle but it was really only a stage on the way to becoming national newspaper journalists and so in 1970 we came to London where Neville had landed a job at the *Daily Telegraph*.

In Newcastle, we were living in a five-bedroom house in Jesmond, the city's prime residential area, and rented out the top floor to students. This paid the mortgage. Although neither of us were earning huge sums on local papers, we managed very well. It was a different story when we came to live in London as there was absolutely nothing we could afford to buy unless we went right out to the suburbs.

Eventually we found a tiny house in The Alberts, Richmond, where I just about went round the bend with two small children, no job and no money. Was I going to be repeating my mother's early postwar years?

For a time, it looked like it. Neville's salary at the *Telegraph* hardly covered our outgoings and it looked as though my life was over, at only 26 years old. I applied for job after job on Fleet Street and was rejected everywhere. At the same time, friends whom I had worked with on local papers were landing national newspaper jobs. I gave myself an ultimatum; that if I didn't get into Fleet Street in a couple of years I would go back to teaching.

Then the dam began to break. First of all I got a staff job on a Mother and Baby magazine. It didn't pay all that well but as Neville was working nights as a sub-editor, he looked after Tom and Will after they got back from play-school until I got home. After I got the sack from that job, just before the magazine folded, I began to get freelance work on national magazines and was eventually earning reasonable money. But the real breakthrough came when I was offered a staff job on the *Sunday People*, a highly successful tabloid then selling more than five million copies a week. Finally, I got there. Our finances doubled overnight and I never really looked back.

Philip Norman was at this time riding high as a star journalist on the *Sunday Times Magazine* and his mother used to come into my mother's shop, where they would exchange stories about these strange children who worked in Fleet Street. One might have expected my mother to be proud of me, a national newspaper journalist against all the odds, but no. When my first book came out, she said: 'Everybody writes books these days.'

I said, 'Do they? How many have you written?' Later she would complain that Smith's didn't have my book, the implication being that it was of so little account that the only bookshop she had heard of wasn't stocking it. I now believe she was jealous of me for escaping, for carving out a life that left her far behind and that is why she did me down—unconsciously—when she had the opportunity. It is a little acknowledged phenomenon that mothers, particularly, do not like their daughters to outshine them, as it highlights the choices they have made. I also, unlike her, got divorced and that was another thing: I had the courage to leave my marriage, which she never did.

She was sad when my marriage ended as she had been fond of Neville and as people used to say, 'As far as she's concerned, the sun shines out of his bum.' But Neville and I stayed friends, and he remained loyal by going to visit her from time to time. Our marriage had to end because Neville, at the time medical correspondent of the *Daily Mail*, had become interested in spirituality and meditation, eventually joining the Brahma Kumaris full-time and going to live in one of their retreat centres. Although I was reasonably sympathetic, the ascetic lifestyle of the BKs never appealed to me and I never took to meditation, either. It was unlikely that either of our families would understand any of this.

Ever since Neville and I met we have argued over whose family was the more dysfunctional, his or mine. His argument was that whereas the dysfunction in my family was blatantly obvious, the dysfunction in his family was hidden. And then, later, a school friend topped us by saying that the dysfunction in her family was both out in the open AND hidden.

Perhaps all families are dysfunctional in their own way and many of us believe that our own was the worst, as that was what we experienced. Onlookers only catch glimpses, while those in the family have to endure the dysfunction day in day out.

Mothers often want their daughters to validate their lives by copying them as closely as they can. In St Neots in the old days, many mothers wanted nothing more than for their daughters to live next door to them. My niece Samantha, Richard's daughter, always said that she admired my mother for having an independent career in the days when it was not so common, and I can see her point. Mum loved her job, her customers and the gossip; that was, until Richard came in and ruined it all. When I asked her why on earth she had taken him into the shop when all he did was to sponge off her, she said: 'I thought I would never hear the last of it if I kept saying no.' I think she knew in her bones that it would never work but in the early days, Richard hardly spent any time in the shop as he was always out rowing.

She complained about him endlessly but knew he would cling on like a limpet, enjoying his free ride. As he got older, he was full of big talk. He was going to open a shop in Bedford; he was going to build his own house, he was 'gonna' do this, 'gonna' do that. Of course, none of it ever happened and my husband and I called him a 'gonna'. Another thing, when Richard's first marriage ended, Samantha went to live with her mother and Sean, his son, lived with him. For decades, the two halves of the family never spoke to each other. Samantha went to university and became a science teacher in a comprehensive school. She married a doctor and they had three children, one adopted. Sean married a Swedish woman and went to live in Sweden where he established a cleaning business (I believe; something like that). The two children of Richard's bitterly broken marriage both did well and their own marriages have lasted.

So perhaps the taint, which seemed so deeply embedded, has worked itself out. All the grandchildren, now adult themselves, seem fine as well. The thing is to extricate oneself from a bad situation, not continue in it. Richard's first and second wives also had the sense to extricate themselves, once it became clear that they had married a kind of monster.

I know that mothers often make lifelong martyrs of themselves looking after their autistic or handicapped children, in the process destroying any independent lives they might have had for themselves, and I'm afraid my mother was one of those. I sometimes wonder how different things might have been if I had been, as she wanted, an only child. But—it's pointless wondering what if.

Our sons Tom and Will would sometimes come to St Neots and remark that everybody looked inbred and that they thought my father and brother were gipsies. They were wary and kept their distance but did say that they thought St Neots was a most peculiar place.

My mother did show some pride when our son Tom graduated from Cambridge University and she was there with my now ex-husband at the ceremony. I was in India at the time, although this was many years before my encounter with Liz Edmunds on the mountaintop that led to the memories being recalled for this present book.

17

The Class Factor

ALTHOUGH NOBODY WAS quite sure where Pauline Sismey fitted into the social hierarchy of St Neots, we did know that she was firmly in the upper echelons. Class divides have formed a staple of British drama from *Upstairs Downstairs* to *Downton Abbey* and *The Admirable Crichton*, but nowhere was the class factor more evident than in the St Neots of the 1950s and 60s.

The town, in those days, had a class structure so rigid that it was almost comical. At the very top was the Rowley family, who owned Priory Park and acres of land all around. By the 1940s, Priory Park was derelict, one of the Rowleys was in a loony bin and another lived in America.

Then came the landed gentry, who mainly occupied large manor houses in surrounding villages. After that came the gentlemen farmers and the rich manufacturing families. Next was the very small professional class which consisted of the solicitors and doctors. There were in my time two firms of solicitors and four doctors, each with their individual practices.

Slightly lower down were the estate agents, auctioneers and dentists and after them came the building firms, shop-owners and bank managers.

Teachers came somewhere here, along with the ministers of religion, who were socially quite difficult to place. Solicitor's daughter

Christian Bevington said that her parents felt they had to invite the Church of England vicar and his wife to their dinner parties, as the vicar was an educated man who had been to Cambridge. He was in their class socially, but not as far as income went. He lived in a huge draughty vicarage which later became an old people's home; that's how big it was.

Down at the bottom came the very largest class of people: the shop assistants, factory workers, lorry drivers, council workers and farm workers; the peasants. These lived at best in council houses, at worst in one of the mean terraced houses with no electricity or indoor sanitation. That is the class that I came from, right down at the lowest rung of the social ladder. But it would be a mistake to assume that the people on this lowest rung were an undifferentiated mass. Tiny gradations that would have been invisible to outsiders marked you out as being a little bit better or a tiny bit worse than your next door neighbour or the family down the street.

In St Neots, your social position was delineated by which shop you bought your shoes, or your coffee. Or even if you drank coffee, as most St Neots people in those days drank tea. Coffee was considered 'posh'. As a child I longed for a pair of shiny black patent shoes but was never allowed to have them because they were to be had at Freeman Hardy and Willis, the 'common' shoe shop, and my shoes had to come from Barrett's, which sold Clark's and Start-Rite.

Similarly, my clothes never came from the Co-op but once again had to come from Barrett's, the local department store. When the first teenage shop, Frances, opened on the High Street, my mother thought it was 'common' and my dresses had to come from Avril's, the more upmarket but less trendy dress shop that took over the premises that had been Paxton Park Nurseries. Dresses from Avril's cost twice as much as those from Frances and naturally, everybody knew the difference. 'Yes, it came from Avril's' was a proud boast.

On Saturdays, mothers and daughters would sometimes catch the bus to Bedford for shopping and when they came back, would be asked: 'Did you go to E.P. Rose's or Rose's in the Arcade?' E.P. Rose, the department store, was the 'posh' shop and Rose's in the Arcade was the 'common' shop. The answer you gave put you in your place as far as your social position went. The smarter mothers and daughters went in the opposite direction, to Cambridge, to buy clothes from Robert Sayle, now a John Lewis, or Joshua Taylor. I can distinctly remember standing at the bus stop waiting to go to Cambridge feeling very superior to the people opposite waiting for the bus to Bedford.

There was also a big divide as to whether you went to 'church' or 'chapel'. 'Chapel folk' who attended the Methodist, Congregational or Baptist Church were looked down on by those who worshipped at the 14th century parish church of St Mary the Virgin. My mother was sorely disappointed when I defected from church to chapel, even though the dissenting churches made far more effort to attract and entertain children than the aloof Anglican church. Another aspect was that the Church of England vicars, in those days, were almost always educated at Oxford or Cambridge, whereas the dissenting ministers may have gone to a nonconformist theological college, or maybe not even that. Even the vicar at a tiny village like Waresley was usually an Oxbridge man. During the 1960s, this was the Rev. Ralph Thicknesse, who was later exposed in the *News of the World* as one of the first 'dirty' vicars; or, at least, one of the first to be outed in a tabloid newspaper. Philip Norman's early novel *Slip on a Fat Lady*, mentions the vicar's daughters, but although they are not named, they are clearly the daughters of Ralph Thicknesse, who had four of them.

And then, did you have a car, a telephone, did you go on holiday? Any of those acquisitions, still relatively rare in the 1950s, would elevate you above your neighbours. Many of my primary school friends never, ever went on holiday but we always did, usually to the nearest seaside place such as Clacton or Skegness. Did you have new clothes at Easter? All self-respecting mothers bought their children a new outfit for Easter but some families simply could not afford new clothes.

There was also the matter of accents as the way you spoke probably marked you out more than anything else. Most people in St Neots spoke with broad Huntingdonshire accents and in order to avert this, any parent who could possibly afford it either sent their children for elocution lessons or to private schools, or both. John Wingate, for instance, would never have dreamed of sending his children to the local council school for fear that they might pick up the local accent. My mother almost totally judged her customers by the way they spoke and anybody who was 'well-spoken', such as Pauline Sismey, got better attention than those who spoke with St Neots accents. She even remarked disparagingly of my cousin Tony's children that they spoke 'a bit Stamford'.

'Well-spoken' people were judged to be more intelligent, richer and worthier of respect than those who dropped their aitches or spoke with a glottal stop, which was almost a criminal offence among the higher and mightier citizens. St Neots born and bred people were actually frightened of those who spoke with educated accents, as the following example will show:

The eleven-plus exam, which all primary school children took, was in two parts. There was the written exam consisting of arithmetic, composition and something called intelligence. (Note: when I looked at the exam papers for 1955, I found I couldn't answer a single question, yet I had passed this very exam with distinction aged 11.) If you passed the written exam, the next step was an interview with the headmaster and senior mistress of Huntingdon Grammar School. Mr Rowntree, MA Cantab, and Mrs Stuart, MA London, spoke with Oxford accents and some children were so nervous of this that they became completely tongue-tied and couldn't answer a single question. They just sat there paralysed with shyness and for this, they were failed. One boy I knew, Barry Jex, was so shy that he simply could not speak and so was failed. Here, the headmaster of the primary school, Mr Cobourne, intervened and wrote a letter to the Director of Education, Ian Currey, to say that he thought this boy was actually grammar school material, but that he was an exceptionally shy child. The intervention worked, Barry was admitted to the grammar school and later became a headmaster himself.

Mr Rowntree and Mrs Stuart often came into my mother's shop after the interviewing was over, and Mum was equally impressed with their accents. 'They are so well-spoken,' she would say, 'it's a pleasure to listen to them.' In addition, they had university degrees, which in the 1950s were rare indeed in St Neots and almost the only person who possessed one was the vicar, the Rev. Canon Leonard Galley who was, once again, a Cambridge man.

These rigid class barriers began to break down with the introduction of the 1940s Education Acts, which gave clever children from poor families, for the first time, the chance of higher education and escape from their lowly origins, completely free. It is not too much of an exaggeration to say that when I passed the eleven-plus and went to Huntingdon Grammar School, nine miles away from St Neots, the attitude of my mother's posh customers, including that of Pauline Sismey, started to change. Gradually, from being completely ignored, I began to be treated with respect. Education made the difference. Along the way I lost my St Neots accent. I knew I would never get anywhere while I spoke pure St Neots, and in fact, it was usual for clever and ambitious working-class children to lose their regional accents. Broadcasters Joan Bakewell and Sue Lawley reckoned their careers would never even have started if they had continued to speak broad Yorkshire or broad Bristol.

When I applied to university, instead of looking down on me as a mere shopkeeper's daughter, my mother's customers started to be in awe of me and called me 'Mrs Garrett's clever daughter'. Some, it is true, thought I was getting above myself but mostly, they realised that society was changing, and they could no longer treat people like me as from a lower order of humanity. But it wasn't just me. Although in the early 1960s it was unusual for a St Neots girl to go to university, it was no longer completely unknown. Joan Ashley, for instance, a stone-mason's daughter, won a scholarship to Somerville College, Oxford and Sheila Clyde, whose single mother worked as a petrol pump attendant, went to London University to read Classics. Christian Bevington, the local solicitor's daughter, went to the London School of Economics and qualified as a barrister but then, she was from the upper reaches anyway.

We were, in fact, leaving those from more privileged backgrounds far behind and striding out in the world armed with our degrees and our new-found confidence. While they stayed in St Neots or round-about, we were making waves in London, or in other countries. We were becoming journalists, lawyers, doctors, television producers ourselves and not just making the tea or running errands. One school friend, Matthew Robinson, became a producer on *Coronation Street* and later, *East Enders*. Colin Croot, a village lad from Waresley, whose father had been a gardener and lived in a tied cottage, won a scholarship to Peterhouse, Cambridge. Grahame Jackson, who lived next door to Pauline in Waresley, studied for a PhD at Imperial College, London.

There was a chance now for clever, ambitious people to get on in life and in the main, they took it. In his memoir *We Danced on our Desks*, Philip Norman bemoaned the fact that he had not been to uni-versity and worried that this would hold him back, as graduate trainee schemes had now been implemented for potential journalists. But he needn't have been concerned; at the age of 22 he was a fêted young writer on the *Sunday Times Magazine* when most graduates were still mouldering away on provincial papers. Philip writes in his memoir about his reaction when his editor first put his name on a story he had written for the *Hunts Post*: 'He'd given me a byline—and an addiction that heroin couldn't have matched.'

In no other era would any of this have been possible. And of course, once we got away from the area we rarely, if ever, went back. There was little scope for people like me in St Neots and Huntingdon. The most I could have hoped for if I had stayed in the area was to be a doctor's receptionist or secretary to an estate agent.

And it was not just in the matter of education that children from poor backgrounds were beginning to be successful. Ivan Twigden left school at 15 with no qualifications. The school's careers officer gave him the choice of being a postman or a builder's labourer. His grand-father had been a postman and also shoe repairer but Ivan took the latter opportunity and ten years later, was a millionaire. For many years he appeared on the *Sunday Times* rich list and he bought one of the grand houses formerly occupied by a gentleman farmer, to live in himself. Ivan became the second biggest private house-builder in the country and now in his 80s, is still working full time and tells me he is 'as fit as a fiddle.'

He said: 'From the start I was always prepared to take risks. In the 1960s, I wanted to borrow three-quarters of a million pounds and that was not easy for an illegitimate lad from a council estate. But eventually I got the loan and it set me on my way. You also have to accept that not everything will work out and be able to ride the downs as well as the ups.'

Ivan failed the eleven-plus exam which in those days was the only way to get an education in St Neots if your parents could not afford to pay for you to go to a private school. What if Ivan had passed the exam? He said: 'If I had gone to the grammar school, I would most likely have become an accountant or a banker and would never have enjoyed the success I have had. As it was, I had my own building company by the age of 21.'

Such rags-to-riches stories are so rare in St Neots that Ivan Twigden is still the only local boy who became so stupendously rich and successful, starting with absolutely nothing. I can remember him bashing tennis balls against the walls of his grandparents' council house for hours and hours, and he also used to take his tennis racket and balls to the railway station, where he would play against himself underneath the arches. It is perhaps not surprising that he became county tennis champion and added to this county table tennis and squash champion. He also founded a riding for the disabled charity, owned racehorses and opened restaurants. 'I just can't stand still,' he said, adding that he was now growing vegetables as well as all his other activities.

In common with many entrepreneurs, Ivan has been married three times and says he now regrets his second marriage. But ever restless, he was on the fast track and he felt he outgrew his first wife once he began to be successful. For many years now, he has hobnobbed with the local gentry and aristocracy and he lives in some splendour in a manor house just outside Kimbolton; in the very next village to Great Staughton in fact. He was able to send all five of his children to fee-paying schools. Although he started off building very modest homes, he now builds top of the range executive houses. 'I always wanted to leave something permanent behind,' he told me, 'and you can't get anything much more permanent than a house.'

Ivan's real-life story reminds me very much of the 1936 Somerset Maugham short story 'The Verger'. In this, Albert Edward Foreman, an illiterate verger in the local church, is given the sack when the new young vicar realises that he can neither read or write. Foreman wanders miserably round the streets wondering what on earth he might do next. Wanting to buy some cigarettes, he comes to a street with no tobacconist's shop. On a whim, he decides to pour his modest savings into opening a tobacconist's and eventually acquires a string of tobacconist's shops. Now a rich man, his banker asks: 'Whatever would you have become if you could read and write?' to which Foreman answers that he would still have been a humble verger.

Sometimes, such a tide in the affairs of men, as Shakespeare wrote, leads on to fortune. Similarly, if Philip Norman had gone to university instead of becoming a teenage reporter on the Hunts Post, it is unlikely that he would have become a celebrity writer on the Sunday Times aged 22.

Christopher Curry, from Little Paxton, became a computer entrepreneur and bought Croxton Park, formerly the ancestral home of Lady Myra Fox. Successful men who did stay in St Neots or roundabout, were buying up and living in the country houses where their parents or grandparents had worked as skivvies. Christopher did not come from such a lowly background as Ivan Twigden as he was privately educated at Kimbolton School but decided to go into industry rather than university. Sometimes, a university education, much prized when I was young, can actually hold you back!

However, I am more than glad that I went to university myself as, one has to admit, these three cases of local boys made good all had one thing in common: they were males. I would have had no chance of becoming an apprentice builder, even if I had wanted to be one, and as for becoming a young reporter on a local newspaper, no chance whatever. All the reporters on the *Hunts Post* were male and the only females employed at the paper were secretaries with no possibility that they might ever become journalists.

University in the 1960s gave a chance to girls and I am so grateful that I took that chance.

But it was clear that roles were being reversed in all kinds of ways. Whereas in the 1950s and 60s, the grand ladies who lived in ivy-clad manor houses looked down on shopkeepers, they were now becoming shopkeepers themselves. Anne Furbank, for instance, who married a local gentleman farmer, Richard Furbank, set up a dress shop in Buckden, a village about two miles from Offord Cluny, and later bought The George Hotel next door. Now, if ever I go to Anne's shop in Buckden, I am one of the upmarket customers. In 1951, Thelma and Estelle Eayrs from St Neots started a designer dress shop in Bedford called D'Arcy and Rosamunde. They made my wedding outfit which cost, I remember £30; a large sum in 1965.

Pauline Sismey herself exhibited such a role reversal when, far from being the glamorous actressy lady who had swept into my mother's shop in a cloud of expensive perfume, she established a fruit and vegetable business from her husband's estate. And now, if she came into the shop it was not to buy something but to sell something.

Richard Edmunds, whose family was friendly with the Sismeys, is an exact contemporary of mine. And yet, when we were children, our paths would never have crossed. This is not meant to imply that Richard was any sort of snob, just that he went to public school, his sister went to boarding school, and there would have been no way that our two families would have socialised together. They knew their place and we knew ours.

If you were to live in St Neots or in the area today, you would not come across any vestige of this class divide that seemed so uncrossable in the past. Far from it.

The vast housing estates that began life with the first of the overspill have obliterated many of the little villages and the stately homes of the past, if they are left standing, go for relatively modest sums. Offord Cluny Manor, for instance, which was sold in 2016 for £1.8 million, is not worth much more than my three-bedroom flat in Oxford. Hilton Hall, near St Ives, which was the home of the Garnett family for about 80 years, went for £1.5 million. These mansions, which once seemed so inaccessible, not only came within our reach, but were affordable at a knockdown price, considering what the same size place would have cost in central London.

As for those stupendously rich Northern industrial families, their vast fortunes, their stately homes and their influence in society have all more or less vanished. The soap factory that lathered the Gossages' and Timmises' fortunes has disappeared; all the manufacturing businesses that once thrived in places like Manchester and Leeds have long gone and, mostly, their families have become ordinary. There are no gentlemen farmers left in Huntingdonshire or, at least, none that you would doff your cap to. The last one to go was Gerald Davison, of Manor Farm, Southoe, who died aged 98 in 2022.

Robin Winterbottom, for instance, went to Eton like his adopted father, but his own children attended the local comprehensive, and his son Paul is a teacher at a local Academy in Aberdeen.

And along with the breaking down of class barriers has gone the stigma of illegitimacy, of adoption, and of the perceived necessity for hiding the truth, even to the extent of inventing fathers and pretending a grandmother was actually the mother. In the past, much was hidden but now, when people write agonised memoirs about how they were abused in childhood—the 'misery memoir' has become a genre in its own right—it may seem as though there are no dark family secrets left uncovered any more.

It is tempting to speculate whether Pauline's life might have been any different if she had not lived a lie for the first 16 years of her life, if her mother had not tried to hide her paternity from her. But then, in 1912, Emma must have felt it necessary to conceal the truth of her daughter's paternity to the extent of inventing a deceased husband, giving herself and her daughter a false name, and doing her utmost to avoid a scandal coming out at Heathfield School. And then, hiding the truth so comprehensively that the facts were not supposed to come out until 2029.

One can say that Emma achieved respectability and a high position in society when she married Prince Nicholas and it seems that from relatively lowly origins, the now Princess Elena started to move quite comfortably in the highest social circles. She rose magnificently to the occasion and herself became quite a grand lady, as can be seen from the photographs on the Cosgrove Hall website.

But at what cost to her daughter? It may seem strange that at the age of five or so, I picked up that Pauline was not quite like the other rich ladies of leisure who came into my mother's shop. There was something—although I did not know the word then—arriviste, parvenu, perhaps—about her as exemplified more than anything else, by the mink coat. The mink coat alone ensured that distance was kept, and nobody could get too close. Perhaps, also, she did not want a too close enquiry into her origins, in case it came out that she was illegitimate, as this was still seen as a stain in the 1950s and 60s, although hardly the child's fault.

One possible explanation as to why I was so fascinated by Pauline is that I did not fit in, either, and at some unconscious level, recognised a fellow outsider. I never seemed to belong to my environment which may be one reason I wanted to get out of St Neots at the earliest possible opportunity and never return. So, I picked up on somebody else who was out of kilter with her surroundings, somebody who did not quite belong; not that any bond was ever established between us.

Although there were some rich women in the area or, more accurately, women married to rich men, none of the others would have ever worn an expensive, prized fur coat just to go shopping in St Neots. It would have been kept in cold storage and only brought out for the grandest occasions, such as a winter society wedding or winter race meeting sitting in the Royal Box. Just by wearing her mink coat to go shopping, exemplifying Lady Montdore's advice to her daughter that if you own a mink coat you need never take it off, Pauline marked herself out because the other golden rule in St Neots in those days was that you must never, ever draw attention to yourself, but rather, do your utmost to be as invisible as possible.

We now know, more or less, the whole story of what happened to Pauline. But I wonder what happened to the mink coat?

As Philip Norman noted, Pauline's true-life story reads 'like Evelyn Waugh with a dash of Nancy Mitford'. And all in St Neots, or round about!

Appendix

IN 2005, Offord Cluny resident Betty Norris recorded an interview about her recollections with the Sismeys, whom she knew for 40 years. Here is an edited transcript:

We lived next to Offord Cluny Manor, so I got to know Colonel and Mrs Sismey very well. How it happened was that my husband Arthur and I were looking for a house in Offord and at the same time Colonel Sismey was looking for a tenant for his cottage in the grounds, which had been a gardener's cottage. We decided to rent the cottage temporarily and it was an arrangement that lasted 40 years. So I got involved with the Sismeys, and they told me their life stories over the years.

The Colonel died in 1993 and he was the last of the line as he had no sons. He had a daughter with his first wife, called Islay, after the Scottish island where they had their honeymoon. He had served in the Army, with the Kings' Royal Rifles. They had some wonderful silver in the house including a silver salver, which was stolen in a burglary. The Colonel told me the loss broke his heart.

He had also served in the Far East. He was divorced from his first wife. She had remarried and gone to live in the Isle of Wight. Pauline, who was his second wife, had lived locally, near St Neots. She was born a Russian Princess, she told me, and her mother was a White Russian. Her brother was head of P and O lines, she said. I asked, 'Really?' 'Yes,' she said. 'P and O was named after us, Pauline and Oliver. P and O.' I knew that wasn't correct as it was P and O liners.' [i.e., Peninsular and Oriental. And no, Yurka was not head of P and O.]

Over the years we talked for hours and hours. Mrs Sismey told me that she had been presented at court and had been to a finishing school in Florence. On the grand piano in their living room was a photo of her being presented at court, wearing a white dress and with lots of plumes.

She said she had been married three times. Her first husband was called Dennistoun-Sword and he had been wounded by the Japanese. He spent some time in a nursing home and was very ill, I understand. She had a son called Robin Winterbottom, and she said she had named him that. When I asked why she would call him Winterbottom, she said it was because she didn't like the name Daubeny. I thought then that there were a lot of nicer surnames she could have chosen.

Robin went to Cirencester Agricultural College after leaving Eton. Colonel Sismey was also educated at Eton.

Mrs Sismey was never early for anything and when she took me out for a meal for my birthday one day after ringing for a taxi service, it was three o'clock in the afternoon. When she rang the local taxi service, she said: 'My man, come and take us out.' She was a great character who betted a lot on horses. She would ring up her bookie and say: Hello, this is me, Mrs Sismey, S for Sugar, I for India, M for Mother, E for Easter and Y for Yes.'

When she wanted to catch a train to London she would ring up the station and say, 'I'm in charge of trains. I'm ringing to see whether you have trains going to London and what time they go. I don't want to stop at Peterborough.'

She loved flowers and gardens and every year went to the Chelsea Flower Show, where she stayed at the English Speaking Union Club—her club, as she told me. The Sismeys had a cat that never went out and it was called Lady Tweedsmuir. Some of the village children thought that Mrs Sismey was a witch and would curse them. They found her very scary, with her long dangly earrings, long cigarette holder and bright red lipstick. Yet when they knocked at the Sismeys' door trick and treating at Halloween, she would always invite them in and give them ginger beer. Everybody thought she was a Russian princess who had fled the Russian Revolution.

Colonel Sismey was very involved in public life. He was an Alderman at Huntingdonshire County Council and wanted the council to buy Hinchingbrooke House, which had belonged to the Montagus. When the sale was successful, he invited Arthur and me in the house to celebrate and opened a bottle of champagne. (Hinchingbrooke House is now Hinchingbrooke School.) The Colonel loved the police force, and he was godfather to many police children.

I remember when Mrs Sismey told me her son was getting married in Scotland. She said she needed a passport and I said, you don't need a passport to go to Scotland and she said, 'Yes you do. I'm going to Cambridge to see about my passport. I don't want to be hijacked. Now, what do I need for Robin's wedding?' She brought out a hat that had moth holes in it and some Pirelli slippers. When I asked what she was going to give him for a wedding present, she said: 'an eel-trap.' 'What's that?' I asked. It was a long wicker basket and she took that on the plane with her to Scotland. She rang up the airport to ask the time of the flight and was told that a bus could take her there.

She said, 'My man, I have no intention of going on a bus. I've never been on a bus in my life.' So she ordered a taxi. She flew to the wedding, I believe, on a private plane.

She loved gardens and opened Offord Cluny Manor gardens to the public on many occasions. The gates were supposed to open at 2pm and hundreds of people would turn up. Then they would have to wait until Mrs Sismey opened the gates. She was always late and always kept people waiting.

There were also tennis afternoons as they had a tennis court in the gardens. She was great fun but once she started talking you couldn't get away from her. I missed her so much when she died in 1980, aged 68, but she left me some money in her Will to buy a car. Then I had to learn to drive.

She told me she had been a Red Cross nurse during the war and was also a barrister-at-law. A lot of interesting people came to visit the Sismeys, people like Lord de Ramsey and also many actors. She said she had been married three times and her second husband was called Daubeny. Sometimes it is true, she did look like a witch. She had a long black cloak which she sometimes wore. On the floor in their drawing room was a huge stuffed tiger which Colonel Sismey told he had caught in India.

Colonel Sismey had a distinctive voice and was very involved in local affairs. He was a governor of Offord school and took a great interest in education. He allowed the members of the Offord and Buckden Fishing Club to fish in the stretch of the river that was in his meadow. During his last years, he had full-time nursing care in Hinchingbrooke Hospital and finally, his daughter took him down to Somerset where she lived. By then he was suffering from dementia. He was born in 1900 and died in 1993, aged 93.

Looking back, they were a couple I was privileged to have known and they were certainly eccentric. But then, I'm fond of eccentric people.

Acknowledgements

MANY PEOPLE WERE generous enough to help with the detective work involved in nailing this story. Most of all, I owe an enormous debt to the superb sleuth Susan Dorey, author of *A Winterbottom Family*. Her genealogical genius was invaluable and I could not have managed without it.

Toby Horton gave me a lot of information regarding George and Penelope Winterbottom and helped to piece together missing links. Prince Yurka's daughter Catherine Horwood-Barwise aided me greatly in my researches and filled in many gaps about the Galitzine family.

The Eton archivist was helpful in giving details of Robin Winterbottom's school and subsequent career and writer Ferdinand Mount, an exact contemporary of Robin's at Eton, also gave useful input.

I must also thank many past and present Waresleyites. Colin Croot, a former head boy of my grammar school, was able to locate the Galitzines' grave in Waresley churchyard by means of parish records and maps. Eleanor Jack and Rod Kerr supplied pictures and newspaper cuttings and John Gillett provided cricketing memories of Colin Dennistoun-Sword. Grahame Jackson, who used to live next door to the Dennistoun-Swords, gave me a wry and telling anecdote about Pauline.

For St Neots memories and stories, I thank Gini Westinghouse, formerly Virginia Walmisley-Dresser, her sister Ann Day, and Christian Bevington.

Paul Harrison, President of the Milton Abbey Association, provided pictures and memories of John Wingate, when he taught at the school before becoming a full-time writer. The incredibly diligent staff at the remarkable Bodleian Library unearthed some interesting newspaper cuttings, particularly about the Old Bailey trial of Victor Hervey, later Sixth Marquess of Bristol.

I could not have completed this book without the amazing help of writer Philip Norman, who knew many of the characters involved and even wrote a novel about them; an amusing work which nearly ended in a serious libel case. Philip encouraged me to rework the story to make it more appealing and it is thanks to him that after incorporating his suggestions, the manuscript was picked up by Anthony Eyre, of Mount Orleans Press.

It all started, though, with an apparent chance encounter on a mountaintop in India and so it remains for me to thank Liz Edmunds, who inadvertently started me on the quest which had so many twists and turns, so many false starts, before the whole thing finally came together.

And just when I thought my search for pictures of Pauline and people associated with her was doomed to failure, suddenly some people turned up trumps. The amazing Claire Cisotti, Picture Editor at the *Daily Mail*, found the picture of Pauline Daubeny, as she then was, striding into the Old Bailey to hear the robbery case against Victor Hervey and his associates. Julie Angell, founder member of the Offords Photos and Memories site (https://www.facebook.com/groups/304565714080823) dug up some wonderful and telling photos of Colonel Sismey and his lady. Julie also sent me the interview with Betty Norris, who knew the Sismeys well.

For such an exotic bolter, Pauline Turner/Galitzine/Daubeny/Dennistoun-Sword/Sismey left very little trace, but I hope that she can now take her rightful place among the adventuresses and femmes fatale—and Russian princesses—of the last century.

Bibliography

Books consulted or quoted include:

Broad, David A: A History of Little Paxton: The Story of a Huntingdonshire
    Village on the Banks of the River Great Ouse D. Broad, 1989
Broderick, Oliver: Waresley My Birthplace Oliver Broderick, 2000
Dorey, Susan: A Winterbottom Family Susan Dorey, 2017
Ellison, Arthur: The Reality of the Paranormal Harrap, 1988
Gillies, Midge: The Barbed-Wire University Aurum Press, 2011
Hudson, Dr Harold: Stanfield Hall Geo. Reeve, Wymondham (no date)
Kramer, Rita: Flames in the Field Michael Joseph, 1995
Knight Bruce, Rory: An Unanchored Heart Mount Orleans Press, 2022
Lemmon, David: Johnny Won't Hit Today: A Cricketing Biography of
    J.W.H.T. Douglas George Allen & Unwin, 1983
Macintyre, Ben: SAS Rogue Heroes Viking, 2016
McLaren, Angus: Playboys and Mayfair Men Johns Hopkins University
    Press, 2017
Mitchell, Stewart: St Valéry and its Aftermath: The Gordon Highlanders
    Captured in France in 1940 Pen and Sword, 2017
Mortimer, Roger: Vintage Roger: Letters from the POW Years Constable,
    2020
Mount, Ferdinand: Kiss Myself Goodbye: The Many Lives of Aunt Munca
    Bloomsbury, 2020
Norman, Philip: Slip on a Fat Lady (later retitled See Him Sweat)
    William Heinemann, 1970
Norman, Philip: We Danced on our Desks Mensch, 2022

Owen, Roderic, with Tristan de Vere Cole: *Beautiful and Beloved: The Life of Mavis de Vere Cole* Hutchinson, 1974

Scriven, Marcus: *Splendour and Squalor* Atlantic Books, 2009

Spence, Lyndsy: *The Grit in the Pearl: The Scandalous Life of Margaret, Duchess of Argyll* The History Press, 2020

Willetts, Paul: *Rendezvous at the Russian Tea Rooms* Constable, 2015

Williams, Maureen: *Horton Hall: Gone But Not Forgotten* Maureen Williams, 2019

BRITISH NATIONALITY AND STATUS OF ALIENS ACT, 1914.

CERTIFICATE OF NATURALIZATION GRANTED TO A MINOR.

Whereas an application has been made for the grant of a Certificate of Naturalization to *PAULINE VINCENT TURNER*,
a minor, alleging with respect to the said *PAULINE VINCENT TURNER*,

the particulars set out below :

And whereas I am satisfied that such a Certificate may properly be granted :

Now, therefore, in pursuance of the powers conferred on me by the said Act, I grant to the said *PAULINE VINCENT TURNER*,

this Certificate of Naturalization, and declare that upon taking the Oath of Allegiance within the time and in the manner required by the regulations made in that behalf she shall, subject to the provisions of the said Act, be entitled to all political and other rights powers and privileges, and be subject to all obligations duties and liabilities, to which a natural-born British Subject is entitled or subject, and have to all intents and purposes the status of a natural-born British Subject.

In witness whereof I have hereto subscribed my name this *24th* day of *January, 1928.*

(Sgd) *Austen Chamberlain*

HOME OFFICE,
LONDON.   *One of His Majesty's Principal Secretaries of State.*

PARTICULARS RELATING TO THE APPLICANT.

Full Name   *PAULINE VINCENT TURNER.*

Address   *34, ST JOHN'S WOOD COURT, ST MARYLEBONE, IN THE COUNTY OF LONDON.*

Trade or occupation   *STUDENT.*

Place and date of birth   *PARIS, FRANCE. 17th MARCH, 1912.*

Nationality   *FRENCH.*

Names and nationality of parents   *HENRY SUTTON TIMMIS, BRITISH, AND EMMA LILIAN HODGSON (KNOWN AS TURNER), BRITISH.*

(FOR OATH
see overleaf.)

TX 1811. 5/21. J. T. & S. Ltd.